Red Star &
Green Dragon:
Looking at
NEW CHINA

Red Star &
Green Dragon:
Looking at
NEW CHINA

Lila Perl

ILLUSTRATED WITH PHOTOGRAPHS

WILLIAM MORROW AND COMPANY
New York   1983

PHOTO CREDITS: All photographs are by Lila Perl with the exception of the following: New China News Agency, p. 66; United Nations, pp. 65, 71 (A. Holcombe), 75. Permission is gratefully acknowledged.

Printed in the United States of America.

1 2 3 4 5 6 7 8 9 10

Library of Congress Cataloging in Publication Data
Perl, Lila.   Red star and green dragon.
Bibliography: p. Includes index. Summary: Reviews recent Chinese history and discusses social, economic, and political factors which influence life in modern China. 1. China—History—1949—Juvenile literature. [1. China] I. Title. DS777.55.P4247 1983   951.05
82-18858
ISBN 0-688-01721-5

Contents

Red Star &
Green Dragon:
Looking at
NEW CHINA

How to Pronounce Pinyin

Pinyin is the Chinese system for writing Chinese words in English. It was developed in 1958 and began to be used officially in 1979. Most words are sounded as they are spelled. But some letters have different sounds:

$q = ch$ Jiang Qing is pronounced *jang ching*.
$x = sh$ Deng Xiaoping is pronounced *deng show-ping*.
$c = ts$ Ci Xi is pronounced *tsee shee*.
$z = dz$ Mao Zedong is pronounced *mow dze-dong*.
$zh = j$ Zhou Enlai is pronounced *jo en-lie*.

Chinese place names that appear in the book are pronounced like this:

Guangxi *(gwong-shee)*
Hangzhou *(hong-jo)*
Ningxia *(ning-shee-a)*
Suzhou *(soo-jo)*
Xian *(shee-an)*
Xinjiang *(shin-jang)*
Wuxi *(woo-shee)*

NOTE: The Pinyin spelling for China's capital, Peking, is Beijing. The Pinyin spelling for the city of Canton is Guangzhou. However, in this book the two cities are referred to as Peking and Canton because those names are most familiar to readers.

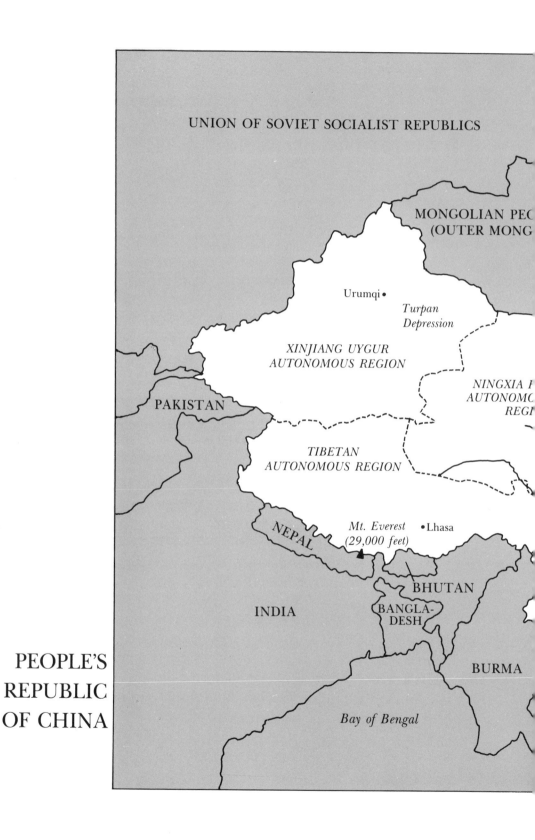

UNION OF SOVIET SOCIALIST REPUBLICS

MONGOLIAN PEC
(OUTER MONG

Urumqi•

Turpan
Depression

XINJIANG UYGUR
AUTONOMOUS REGION

NINGXIA F
AUTONOMC
REGI

PAKISTAN

TIBETAN
AUTONOMOUS REGION

Mt. Everest   •Lhasa
(29,000 feet)

NEPAL

BHUTAN

INDIA   BANGLA-
DESH

PEOPLE'S
REPUBLIC
OF CHINA

BURMA

Bay of Bengal

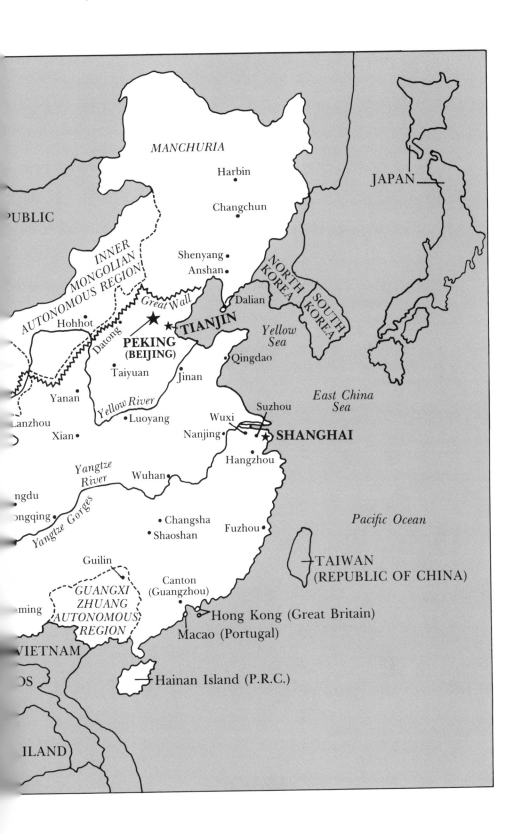

MANCHURIA

Harbin •

Changchun •

•PUBLIC

INNER MONGOLIAN AUTONOMOUS REGION

Shenyang •
Anshan •

Great Wall

NORTH KOREA

SOUTH KOREA

JAPAN—

Dalian •

Hohhot •

★ ★ **TIANJIN**

Yellow Sea

Datong •

PEKING (BEIJING)

Taiyuan •

• Qingdao

Jinan •

Yanan •

Yellow River

East China Sea

Lanzhou •

• Luoyang

Wuxi • Suzhou

Xian •

Nanjing • ★ **SHANGHAI**

Yangtze River

Wuhan •

Hangzhou •

ngdu

ongqing •

Yangtze Gorges

Pacific Ocean

• Changsha
• Shaoshan

Fuzhou •

Guilin •

—TAIWAN (REPUBLIC OF CHINA)

GUANGXI ZHUANG AUTONOMOUS REGION

Canton (Guangzhou) •

ming

Hong Kong (Great Britain)

Macao (Portugal)

VIETNAM

OS

•Hainan Island (P.R.C.)

ILAND

One of the many royal palaces in Peking's Forbidden City, so named because commoners were forbidden to enter it.

CHAPTER ONE

The Dragon Throne

For thousands of years China was a country locked in mystery. In early times, only a few adventurous travelers visited it. They brought back almost unbelievable tales.

The Chinese, they said, knew how to weave a marvelous, shimmering fabric out of threads spun by fat, white worms. The Chinese had invented sheets of thin, flexible, pale-colored material on which one could write or paint. They knew how to combine certain mineral substances that could explode, causing dense smoke and a huge amount of noise.

Centuries passed. During the Middle Ages, Europeans became more and more curious about the distant Asian land that was then called Cathay. Traders attempted to reach it in order to bring back silks, spices, and jewels.

Marco Polo was the son of an Italian merchant family from the city of Venice. During his life, he spent many years in China. Traveling with his father and his uncle, he left home in 1271 and did not return until 1295. He found that China was ruled by an emperor of enormous wealth and power. Later when he wrote about the sumptuous life at the Chinese court, about the bustling cities and the roads and canals that linked them, people did not believe him.

They found it difficult, too, to believe Marco's account of his amazing caravan journey from the Near East to China. We still wonder how the Polos survived the overland trek across Asia to the Chinese capital of Peking, which Marco called Cambaluc.

Their caravan route took them over chill, barren mountains and through burning deserts. These wild, forbidding borderlands had kept China almost completely sealed off from the West. To the east, China was protected from visitors by the vast Pacific Ocean, which often brought howling coastal typhoons. The sailing ships of long ago could not easily make the hazardous journey. Even after the travels of Marco Polo, China continued to remain isolated from Europe and Europeans for hundreds of years.

The Chinese were content with this state of affairs. They called their country the Middle Kingdom, for they thought of it as the center of civilization. They believed that the Earth was square and flat and that the fringes of their domain were inhabited by crude and barbaric peoples. One of their emperors boasted that his Celestial Empire did not need or want anything from beyond its borders. And it was true that China was richly self-sufficient.

The Chinese can trace their civilization back for 2000 years before the birth of Christ. About that time they formed their first kingdom headed by a succession of rulers from the same family. This inherited line was known as a dynasty. Even in such early times, Chinese artisans were making both useful and beautiful objects out of pottery, bronze, jade, and wood.

Around 1300 B.C. the Chinese invented a system of writing. They used picture drawings, called pictographs, to form words. These pictures gradually became the tens of thousands of Chinese characters that exist today. Most Chinese who read and write, however, know only about two thousand

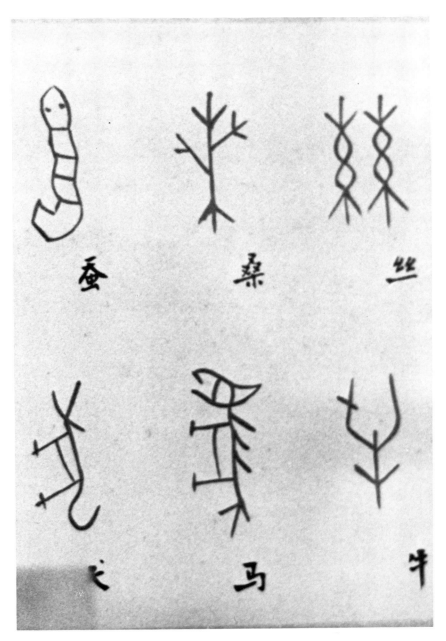

Early picture writing that led to the Chinese written characters. From left to right, the top row reads: silkworm, mulberry tree, silk skeins.

of the most commonly used characters. Scholars know ten thousand or more.

At first the Chinese carved their picture writing onto animal bones or slips of bamboo. But around A.D. 100 they discovered a way to make paper out of pounded fibers of wood or cloth. They also developed ink and writing brushes. Later, they even invented a system of printing using carved wooden blocks or pieces of molded clay.

China probably takes its name from a dynasty called the Qin (pronounced *Chin*), which came to power in 221 B.C. By then China had become divided into many small kingdoms, each one trying to gain control of the others. The Qin ruler succeeded in conquering and uniting the warring states, and formed them into an empire.

As his new domain was now very large, the emperor, whose name was Qin Shi Huang, tried to establish a strong central government. He also started to standardize several aspects of Chinese life.

Qin Shi Huang, the first ruler of the Chinese empire.

Qin issued a great many decrees. He ordered that all the money in the country had to be in the form of round coins with square holes in their centers. Before that the various kingdoms had used coins shaped like knives, spades, and other objects. The written forms of the Chinese characters were standardized throughout the empire, and so were all the weights and measures. Even the axle lengths of the carts and wagons had to be made uniform so that the wheel ruts in all the muddy country roads of China would be exactly the same size.

One of Qin Shi Huang's greatest achievements was the Great Wall of China. True, long before the Qin Dynasty came to power, many separate walls had already been built by the smaller kingdoms to keep out the northern invaders who swept down from the plains of Mongolia. The Mongols were bold horsemen who often raided the carefully cultivated farmlands of northern China, stealing livestock, looting, and taking captives.

Qin Shi Huang decided that all the defensive walls should be linked together to form one great wall that would wind its way across the tops of the rugged northern mountains like a huge stone dragon. Many thousands of Chinese workers were recruited to build the tall fortification of earth and rocks with its notched parapet and stone sentry towers. Through slitlike openings in these structures, sharpshooter archers would be able to aim their arrows at the enemy.

When the work was completed, the Great Wall extended for over 1400 miles. Later rulers strengthened and improved the wall with bricks and shaped stone. Its average height is 25 feet, and on its crest it has a roadway of paving blocks wide enough so that five horses or ten people can march abreast. It is not surprising that the Great Wall of China is the only human structure on Earth that can be seen from space!

(Above) The Great Wall of China snaking its way over the crests of the mountains. (Below) Crowds of schoolchildren and other sightseers visiting the Great Wall.

Before he died, the emperor Qin Shi Huang did an extraordinary thing. He planned to have himself buried with an entire life-size army of 8000 warriors, servants, and horses. The figures were made of terra cotta (clay that is hardened and painted like pottery), and each soldier was modeled with a different face, expression, body shape, and hair style, exactly as in real life. In the past, Chinese rulers had often had living soldiers, horses, wives, and court officials buried with them in their tombs. But perhaps Qin felt more secure with an army that would not soon be reduced to rotted flesh and moldering bones.

One of the life-size terra cotta warriors of the Qin emperor.

When the huge underground tomb at Qin's capital near the city of Xian was accidentally discovered in 1974, his army was still ranked in formation like a standing honor guard. Although some of its weapons had been stolen by grave robbers, probably around the time of burial, many of the archers still held real bows and arrows; the swordsmen still carried sharp, glittering swords and spears.

In 1980 another huge earth mound near the unopened grave of the emperor himself was excavated. It revealed bronze horses, chariots, and charioteers. These were the largest bronzes ever cast in imperial China.

Inside Qin's own burial area, there is said to be a replica of China in miniature, with models of richly fashioned palaces, quicksilver rivers, gold and silver birds, and trees carved out of jade. The writings of an ancient Chinese historian tell us that the emperor's body was placed in a dragon-shaped sarcophagus, lamps of whale oil were left burning, and mechanically set bows and arrows were placed near the entryways, aimed so that they would pierce the body of any would-be intruder. The Chinese rulers made lavish preparations for their afterlife, while poor people did not even expect to have a life after death.

Amazingly, for all its wealth, power, and accomplishment, the dynasty founded by Qin Shi Huang lasted only a few years beyond his death, and a mere fourteen years in all. The harshness of his rule and the heavy taxes he imposed brought on widespread rebellion. The people remembered the untold thousands of slave laborers who had died of exhaustion during the building of the Great Wall. Neither did they forget Qin's many cruel punishments—on one occasion, the emperor had had four hundred scholars buried alive because they disagreed with his policies.

Nevertheless, the Chinese empire did last for 2100 years,

through many more dynasties. The following dynasty, the Han, held power for over 400 years. It was during this period that paper was invented and the first paper money anywhere began to circulate throughout the empire. Also under the Han, the dragon became the official symbol of the emperor.

Sculpted bronze figures of the founders of the Han Dynasty, on view in the Nanjing Museum.

The dragon is a mythical creature. It is often pictured as having the head of a fanged beast, claws, wings, and the long, slithering, scaly body of a serpent. In Chinese mythology, however, this ugly monster represents not only the godly power of the emperor but is also thought to bring good fortune. Images of dragons adorned carvings, sculpture, and painted decorations at the royal court and were embroidered onto the silken robes of the wealthy.

A dragon carved atop a wall in the famous Yu Garden in Shanghai.

The Han Dynasty also gave its name to the Chinese people. About 94 percent of the country's population today is made up of Han, or "true" ethnic Chinese. The remaining 6 percent are non-Han minority peoples. Some like the Mongols, the Manchurians, and the Tibetans have Oriental features. But others, like the Uygur who inhabit the far northwest of modern China, look more like Europeans. It was, of course, to keep out the non-Han Mongol peoples that the Great Wall was originally built.

Probably one reason for the long rule of the Han Dynasty was its acceptance of the teachings of Confucius, a set of beliefs that many Chinese followed. Confucius, who lived from 551 B.C. to 479 B.C., taught that both the family and the state must be based on fixed relationships of loyalty and respect. In the family, the son must respect the father, the wife the husband, and the younger brother the older brother. Outside the family, friend must be loyal to friend. And the citizens of the nation must respect and obey their ruler, who was called the son of heaven. These were known as the five relationships.

The Chinese practice of ancestor worship probably grew out of these Confucian ideals. Many homes, no matter how humble, had altars holding wooden tablets on which the names of ancestors were inscribed. To honor their forebears, eldest sons would burn incense and make offerings before the altars. Younger sons were not considered worthy enough to perform such ceremonies, while women and girls had the fewest rights and privileges in the family.

On the government level, Confucianism worked very well as a means of preserving harmony, order, and the veneration of the emperor. Chinese historians believe that the early downfall of the Qin Dynasty was due to the emperor's low regard for Confucianism. While demanding dictatorial powers, Qin Shi Huang destroyed many of Confucius's writings. The scholars whom he buried alive had, in fact, been followers of Confucius.

Under the Han Dynasty, the empire expanded and a class of scholar-officials known as mandarins became very important in Chinese society. The mandarins were wealthy landowners. At the same time, they were scholars who held a monopoly on education, for only people with money and leisure could afford to spend the time it took to learn the ten thousand Chinese characters and so master China's classical literature.

As government officials under the Han, the mandarins were in charge of public works such as roads, canals, dams, irrigation, and the storage of grain against times of famine. They were so highly regarded, both as administrators and scholars, that they were the top rank of the four classes of Chinese society. Even the principal dialect of China, originally spoken mainly in the north, is named Mandarin after this elite group.

The other three classes were the farmers, the artisans, and the merchants. Farmers were considered next in importance because they were the producers of the food, clothing, and other goods that were essential to the society. Some farmers had their own land and others rented from the rich landowners. Artisans came next because they were the processors of many of the raw materials the farmers produced. Merchants held the lowest position because they produced nothing, merely exchanging the goods of others for money. Yet, in reality, the merchants often profited the most while the small, hardworking farmers and artisans remained desperately poor.

Two additional classes were considered so lowly as to be beneath the bottom rung of the social ladder. They were the soldiers and the "mean people." Soldiers were recruited from the poorer classes of society. Many soldiers took advantage of the unarmed farmers and shopkeepers, and gained a reputation for looting, burning, and killing. They were also looked down upon because, in spending so much time away from home, they failed to fulfill their family duties as sons, brothers, fathers, or, if they were elder sons, as worshippers of their ancestors.

The "mean people" were the entertainers, prostitutes, and slaves who, again, did not fit into the Confucian order of things. For some reason barbers, too, were included in this underclass.

Because of the strong hold of Confucianism, the Chinese class system, with the mandarins at the top, continued as the pattern of Chinese society until the fall of the empire in 1911. A dynasty often was removed from power because its ruler and its scholar-officials demanded too many luxuries, raised taxes too high, failed to maintain roads and dikes, or did not set aside reserves against a severe drought, flood, earthquake, or other natural disaster. At such times, the soldiers would desert and take to banditry. The peasants would rebel, and the dynasty would be toppled.

But a new one always arose, often headed by a rebel leader. The Confucian system would be reinstated, order would return, and the whole cycle would begin all over again.

The Chinese empire reached its golden age under the Tang Dynasty. The Tang rulers came to power in A.D. 618 and reigned for nearly 300 years. Trade and commerce, art, music, literature, and scholarship all flourished as never before.

Within the country, the 1200-mile Grand Canal had been dug and completed between 589 and 618. This feat was almost as marvelous as the building of the Great Wall, and the result was far more useful. While the wall had by now fallen into disrepair and often failed to repel the Mongol raiders, the Grand Canal served as a smooth, watery highway, linking northern China with the cities and farms of the lush, rice-growing Yangtze River delta in the south.

Today this great waterway, which reaches from Peking to Hangzhou and is fed by hundreds of smaller canals, still bustles with activity. In cities like Wuxi and Suzhou, people live and trade along its banks, and many families dwell on the houseboats and barges that ply its waters.

Under the Tang rulers, the tropical coasts of southern China were explored for their stands of shipbuilding timber, their camphor, cinnamon, incense, and new varieties of wild-growing tea. Tea had become a popular drink in China several hundred years earlier. In the warm south, it was also possible to grow bananas, tangerines, and lichee nuts to de-

The busy waterway of the Grand Canal as it passes through the city of Wuxi.

Aboard a barge that plies the Grand Canal.

light the nobility of the north, and to gather the brilliantly
colored iridescent feathers of tropical birds for royal fans and
headdresses.

The Chinese now traded more beyond their borders and
their arts began to show the influences of objects from southeast Asia, Persia, India, and Arabia. Tang pottery was notable
for its figures of horses and camels glazed in many colors.
During the reign of the Tang, the natural stone of many of
China's cliffs, caves, and grottoes was exquisitely carved with
forms of the Buddha and his disciples. And Buddhist temples
were adorned with statuary and rich decoration.

Buddhism had come to China from India hundreds of
years earlier, but it reached its greatest acceptance at this
time. Gautama Buddha, who formulated the religion, had
lived during the same period as Confucius; but the two sets

of beliefs did not generally come into sharp conflict in China. Perhaps this was because Confucianism was basically a system of social order, while Buddhism was a teaching that helped its followers to seek self-knowledge, peace, and enlightenment. The main goal of Buddhists was to learn how to escape from suffering and reach a state of bliss.

Taoism was still a third belief that had many followers in imperial China. Its founder, Lao-tze, lived about the same time as Confucius, in the sixth century B.C. This religion stresses the need for humankind to return to a state of harmony with the universe by withdrawing from instability, war, and the struggle for power.

Because of its long-lasting influence on the form of the Chinese state, Confucianism was probably the most important of the three faiths. It was responsible, for example, for the "examination system," which had been started under the Han and was strengthened during the Tang. The examination system was intended to preserve order and continuity in the government of China. Under this system, it was believed possible for anybody, even a lowly barber's son, to rise to the position of a scholar-official simply by taking and passing the required civil-service examinations. However, it was rare indeed for such a thing to happen. How could a poor student ever attain the education necessary to pass?

In reality, the examination system served to keep the wealthy, well-educated bureaucrats of the mandarin class entrenched in their positions near the very top of the social pyramid. At the top, of course, was the emperor.

It was also during the Tang Dynasty that the custom of binding women's feet began. This practice became even

A figure of the Buddha surrounded by angels and disciples, in the Jade Buddha Temple, Shanghai.

more widespread under the Song Dynasty, which took power in 960 and lasted for over 300 years. The Song era was also one of great artistic achievement, especially in poetry, painting, and calligraphy, or Chinese brush writing. Exquisite porcelain ware was produced during this period, and the Chinese folk arts of paper cutting and kite, parasol, and lantern making all flowered.

Song Dynasty garden once the property of a wealthy mandarin, today open to the public.

A pair of folk paper cuts. Each picture is painstakingly cut out by hand from a single sheet of black or colored paper.

Unfortunately, in this age of elegance, one of the standards of female beauty was tiny feet. Among the wealthier classes, girls had their feet tightly bound from the age of four or five. By the time they reached their early teens, after having suffered years of intense pain, their feet were only about half the normal size. They were so deformed that some girls could walk only with a hobbling gait, while others stumbled about or were actually forced to crawl. Many women of very poor families escaped foot-binding, for with crippled feet it was almost impossible to do heavy household and farm work. But among other classes even a plain-faced girl could get a husband if her feet were small enough.

After marriage, the woman with bound feet was almost a prisoner in her own home. This cruel practice served to enforce her obedience to her husband and other male members of the household, as originally dictated by the Confucian ideal.

Foot-binding was only one evidence of the low status accorded to women in imperial China. Females were so little valued that in very poor families girl babies might be strangled at birth. Or if a family fell on hard times, a girl child might be sold into slavery or prostitution.

Marriages among both rich and poor were family arranged and based on convenience, money, or social standing. A young girl might be betrothed to an old man, or a young woman to a male infant. Much depended on the year in which the partners were born. Chinese years have the names of various animals, such as dog, pig, rat, bull, dragon, rooster. There are twelve in all. In the Chinese belief, a man born in the Year of the Lamb should not marry a woman born in the Year of the Tiger, for symbolically the wife might swallow the husband.

Wives had to show their subservience by walking ten paces behind their husbands in public. If a man was displeased with his wife, he might take one or more concubines, or mistresses. Upon becoming a widow, a woman might even be buried alive with her dead husband, as was often the case for the emperor's wives and concubines. Not until after the fall of the empire and the onset of the Chinese Communist revolution in the first half of the twentieth century were ideas concerning the equality of women put into action.

The power of the Song Dynasty gradually weakened, and now a dramatic change occurred in China. The Mongols, who had been threatening the fortifications of the empire for over a thousand years, actually became its new rulers. Their dynasty was known as the Yuan and it held sway from 1279 to 1368.

Over the centuries, the Mongol nomads who lived on the vast, windswept plains north of the Great Wall had formed into strong marauding armies. They still herded sheep, goats, camels, and oxen, raised ponies, and lived in yurts. These easily transported dwellings were dome-shaped tents made of felt thrown over a framework of sticks. Unlike the Chinese, their diet included milk, mainly in the form of kumiss, or fermented mare's milk.

Under their renowned leader Genghis Khan, the Mongols swept across Asia, forming an empire that included Russia, Siberia, and parts of India, Persia, and China. Genghis Khan's grandson, Kublai Khan, completed the conquest of China and extended its borders all the way into southeast Asia. For the first time in China's history, a "barbarian" people ruled over the Han Chinese.

It was during Kublai Khan's reign that Marco Polo visited China and was received at the Mongol emperor's court at Peking. Trade between China and other parts of the world expanded, and because the emperor was curious about foreigners, he even welcomed some Christian missionaries from Europe to China.

The Mongols, however, were poor administrators. They abandoned the examination system so that Mongol office-holders could replace Chinese officials. Corruption was widespread, and even during Marco Polo's stay rebellions were frequent. By the time the Polos had completed their lengthy sea voyage back to Venice in 1295, Kublai Khan had died. Soon a Han Chinese rebel leader, who had once been a Buddhist monk, drove the Mongols out of China and declared himself the first emperor of a new dynasty, the Ming.

During this dynasty, the dragon throne was reestablished, first at the city of Nanking, or Nanjing, which means southern capital, and later at Peking, or Beijing, meaning northern

The rebel leader who overthrew the Mongols and became the first Ming emperor.

capital. After a short time, foreign trade was discouraged. The Ming emperors returned the government to the old Confucian traditions and withdrew inside their Middle Kingdom. They hoped never again to have anything to do with "foreign barbarians" from near or far.

CHAPTER TWO

"Blue-Eyed Barbarians"

Silk and porcelain; paper and printing; cast iron and gunpowder; clockworks, spinning wheels, waterwheels, the magnetic compass—all had been developed in China during its long years of isolation.

The Chinese were far ahead of the rest of the world in many of their discoveries and inventions. Their engineers were experts at digging canals, building dams and bridges, and setting up irrigation systems to water their fields. They also built exquisite palaces and temples.

While Europeans were still hacking at their food with hunting knives or tearing it apart with their fingers, the Chinese were already eating with chopsticks. The European fork, in fact, was not invented until the late 1500's, a thousand years after chopsticks had come into use in the Middle Kingdom.

No wonder that ever since the time of Marco Polo the Chinese had looked upon Europeans as "blue-eyed barbarians." As with all foreigners, the Chinese considered the few European traders and merchants who reached their country an inferior people. Those who were permitted to come to

(Above) Examples of the famed blue-and-white Ming porcelain, now in the Nanjing Museum. (Right) The exquisite Temple of Heaven in Peking built by the Ming Dynasty. The emperor prayed there each year for a good harvest.

court had to kowtow, to kneel and knock the ground with their foreheads many times, as a sign of respect for the emperor. The English word "kowtow" comes from the Chinese.

However, during the nearly 300 years that the Ming Dynasty ruled China, great changes began to take place in Europe. The period known as the Middle, or Dark, Ages came to a close and gave way to an era of rebirth in the arts and great advances in the sciences. Shipbuilding and navigation were improved and new sea routes were explored. Columbus discovered America, and one of Magellan's ships completed a voyage around the world, proving once and for all that the Earth was round and not flat as the Chinese supposed.

By 1557 the Portuguese had set up a trading post at Macao, on the southern coast of China. Bearded European sailors came ashore in China for the first time. They were astonished at what they saw. They were baffled by the language, appearance, and customs of the Chinese. China seemed to them a place where everything was done backwards. In Chinese names, the last name appeared first. In a Chinese meal, the soup was eaten last.

The Chinese were not very favorably impressed with the newcomers either, and they limited them so that they could trade only at the ports of Macao and Canton. Nevertheless, the Ming emperor did permit an Italian missionary, the blue-eyed and curly-bearded Father Mateo Ricci, who had arrived in Canton in the late 1500's to later come to the court in Peking. Unlike most European visitors of his day, Father Ricci had taken the trouble to learn Chinese. He was also very sensitive to the feelings of his hosts. Although he brought with him maps of the world, he did not press the Chinese to accept the idea that the Earth was a globe. He allowed them to believe that the Middle Kingdom was still its center.

The emperor and the scholar-officials were delighted to learn from Father Ricci about European clockmaking, astronomy, architecture, and engineering. He, in turn, praised the rich artistic output of the Ming era—its blue-and-white patterned porcelain, ivory carving and inlay work, paintings, and bronzes. Father Ricci was also impressed with the marvelous fireworks displays that were given on festival occasions, filling the sky with brilliant, fiery patterns in many different images and colors. As a European, he was surprised that the Chinese, who had invented gunpowder, should use it so little for purposes of warfare and so much for public celebrations.

Father Ricci was observing something rather important about the China of his day. Its great civilization was more

A pair of seated camels on the pathway leading to the tomb of the first Ming emperor in Nanjing.

concerned with scholarship and the arts than with science and technology. Already China's guns and cannon were far inferior to those being developed in the West. Unfortunately, the West would soon begin to use its advanced firepower to force the rulers of the Celestial Empire to meet its demands for trade and other privileges.

During the next—and last—dynasty, imperial China and the West would come into deep conflict. The Qing (pronounced *Ching*), which took power in 1644, was the second non-Han dynasty to control China. Once again conquest had come from the north. This time it was not the Mongols, however, but a Manchurian people called the Manchus.

The Manchus succeeded in conquering all the territory of the Mings and also expanded their holdings to include Mon-

*The Manchu conqueror of
the Ming Dynasty.*

golia, parts of Russia and Siberia, and Tibet. They tried to
impose their customs on the Han. One of them was the
wearing of the pigtail. The Manchus usually shaved the front
part of the head and grew the rest of their hair long from the
crown, plaiting it into a single braid that hung down the back.

Now they demanded that the Han Chinese—who usually
wore their hair loose or tied in a knot—do the same as a sign
of loyalty to the new regime. As resistance was dangerous,
some Chinese still loyal to the departed Mings took to wearing a pointed straw hat with a false pigtail attached to the
back. Underneath the ko hat, as it was called, was their own
hair tightly bound into a knot.

Although the Qing Manchu Dynasty gained the upper
hand over most of its enemies within the empire, the threats
from the "blue-eyed barbarians" of Europe kept mounting.
During the reign of the Emperor Qian Long in the 1700's,

British, French, Dutch, and Portuguese trading ships called frequently to buy tea, silk, porcelain, and other Chinese products that were in great demand in Europe. In turn, they tried to force the Chinese to buy European goods. But the emperor declared that China's rich civilization wanted nothing from the West.

The British were particularly annoyed at having to pay in silver for their huge cargoes of Chinese imports such as tea, which had become a tremendously popular drink in Great Britain. As the British were already colonial masters in India, they did manage to sell the Chinese some Indian cotton goods. But they needed to find a product for which there would be far greater demand. They eventually thought of selling the Chinese opium, a drug obtained from the opium poppy that was widely grown in India.

Although opium smoking had been declared illegal by the Chinese government in 1729, the popularity of this dangerous narcotic began to grow. The British were pleased at the profit they were soon making from the sale of opium and the improvement in their balance of trade.

By the first half of the 1800's, China was being drained of both goods and currency to pay for the opium shipments, and its society was undergoing corruption and decay as a result of the widespread drug traffic. In desperation, the emperor's representative wrote a letter to Queen Victoria of Great Britain in 1839, begging her to halt the illegal trade. When nothing was done, the Chinese commissioner at Canton took matters into his own hands. He had 20,000 chests of newly arrived opium mixed with quicklime and dumped into the sea.

The British were outraged. They claimed that their trading rights were being interfered with, and they attacked the forts at Canton. They gained an easy victory over the weak military defenses of the Chinese in this so-called First Opium War. In 1842, as the spoils of war, they demanded and got five new trading ports in addition to Canton. One of these was Shanghai. The British also received the island of Hong Kong. Adding insult to injury, they forced the Chinese government to pay heavily for the opium that had been destroyed.

Other Western nations, including the United States, now saw how weak and helpless the Chinese empire really was. They were quick to demand entry to Chinese ports, special trading privileges, and territorial rights. In the last half of the 1800's, Russia and Japan received similar rights that entitled them to these "spheres of influence" in China. The Qing rulers were forced to agree to many unequal treaties simply because their military strength was no match for the foreign gunboats that now sailed up China's rivers and the foreign garrisons now stationed on its soil.

A scene in modern Shanghai. This city was one of the trading ports opened to Great Britain after the First Opium War.

Even Japan, China's neighbor to the east, was building a modern military machine. The island nation had realized the importance of modern technology soon after the first Westerners had appeared on its shores. But China, vast and far-reaching, steeped in its Confucian traditions, had lain like a sleeping giant. Now it appeared to be paying the price for its years of isolation and its long-term refusal to deal with foreigners.

The foreigners whom the Chinese people came in contact with most widely were missionaries from the United States and Europe, representing various religious denominations. Their goal was to convert the Chinese "heathens" to Christianity. Neither Buddhism, Taoism, nor Confucianism with its ancestor worship seemed like proper religions to the Westerners. Besides, the missionaries felt they had a special contribution to make because they were rich enough to open hospitals and schools. With these institutions they were able to bring Western medicine to the Chinese and teach them Western languages along with the Christian bible. Christianity spread mainly in and around the cities, as the Chinese were drawn to the missions seeking relief from hunger and disease.

Most of the missionaries who went to China in the wake of their countries' merchant ships and gunboats were sincere, hardworking, and very helpful to the Chinese. Yet, seeing everything from the Western point of view, they failed truly to understand China's culture and often to respect its traditions.

The Chinese, in turn, wondered why the missionaries could not or would not do anything to stop the opium trade being actively carried on by their own countrymen. Neither could they understand how the missionaries could stand by while their nations' troops looted and burned priceless Chi-

nese property like the twelfth-century imperial Summer Palace outside Peking. This incident took place at the time of the Arrow War of 1856–1860, sometimes known as the Second Opium War. British and French detachments attacked the palace complex because the Chinese government had hesitated too long before signing still another unequal treaty.

Missionaries, like all other Westerners, were not subject to Chinese law. If a foreigner beat or even killed a Chinese, it was up to officials of his own government to bring charges and decide the punishment. In important port cities like Shanghai, entire sections became foreign territory on Chinese soil. The British, French, and other Western powers built their own banks and warehouses, hotels and clubs, parks and racetracks. These "foreign concessions" were reserved for Westerners, and to make this very clear, signs were hung that read *No dogs or Chinese.*

If the Chinese were despised and belittled at home, an even worse fate awaited them when they were sent abroad. Foreigners who visited China saw its people as a good source of cheap labor. So they began arranging for gangs of Chinese laborers to be sent to British and other colonial possessions to work on sugar and rubber plantations. Some Chinese went voluntarily, hoping to make enough money in a few years to return home rich. But many were shanghaied, or kidnapped. The English word "shanghai" comes from the Chinese city of that name. The Chinese were drugged or plied with drink and then put aboard a ship bound for a foreign destination. Whether they left of their own accord or not, most never returned.

Chinese laborers immigrated to California in large num-

An immense gilded Buddha in Hangzhou's Lingyin Temple. Foreign missionaries tried to convert Chinese Buddhists to Christianity.

bers during the mid-1800's to work in the goldfields and help build the railroads. The gang bosses welcomed them because they could be paid less than other workers and forced to work harder. At the same time, they were looked down upon as a "subhuman" race, able to survive on a few pennies a day. Many Americans tagged them the "yellow peril" because they took jobs away from Caucasians. They were often insulted and sometimes brutally attacked by mobs. One of the less violent forms of attack was to cut off a Chinese's pigtail. By the 1880's, feeling against the Chinese ran so high in the United States that the government began passing laws to prevent any more from entering the country.

However, not all Chinese were as long-suffering as the many victims of these times. In China, between 1850 and 1864, a massive rebellion took place that divided the northern and southern halves of the empire into two separate domains.

The revolt, known as the Taiping Rebellion, was led by a Christian convert from Canton named Hong Xiuchuan. The missionaries who had converted Hong some years earlier had not realized how strong their influence would be, for he became convinced that he was the younger brother of Jesus Christ and therefore "the younger son of God the Father."

Gathering a following of other Chinese Christians, Hong set forth on his "God-given mission" to overthrow the Manchus, destroy China's ancient religions of Buddhism and Taoism, and stamp out the Confucian system and the scholar-officials. He saw China's traditions as its greatest enemy and laid the blame for its troubles on the Qing rulers rather than on the Western powers.

At a time when almost no one had yet heard of communism, the Taipings tried to establish a communistic society to be run on the principle of Christian love. Private property

Hong Xiuchuan, leader of the Taiping Rebellion.

was to be abolished and all would share in the nation's wealth. Women would become fully equal with men. Foot-binding, prostitution, and the taking of concubines would be outlawed. The penalty for selling or smoking opium would be death.

The Taipings were in many ways remarkable for they were far ahead of their times. Women fought alongside men in their armies of peasants and laborers. By 1853, they controlled most of southern China and set up their headquarters at Nanjing. That city remained the capital of the Taiping Heavenly Kingdom for the next eleven years.

In the end, the Taiping regime was toppled not by the Manchu rulers in Peking, but by the self-seeking Western powers. The "blue-eyed barbarians" knew that they could get many more concessions for trade and territory from the weakened Manchus than from the fiercely idealistic Taiping leaders. Besides, the Westerners were furious with the Taipings for trying to ban the profitable opium trade. Also, they did not approve of the Taipings' communistic ideas for society.

Many Chinese were hostile to the Taipings, too, because they persecuted Buddhists and Taoists and tried to force them to convert to Christianity. Trapped between enemies of both the East and the West, the Taiping Rebellion proved a lost cause. Upon the defeat of his Heavenly Kingdom, Hong committed suicide.

Although the Taipings were no longer a threat to the Manchu rulers in Peking, events continued to worsen for the Chinese empire. During the closing years of the 1800's, foreign powers with superior military strength bit off great chunks of the Qing domain. Southeast Asia, or Indochina, which had long paid tribute to Peking, was taken by France. Burma became a British possession. Russia moved into Manchuria.

But the deepest blow to China came from Japan. As a result of China's defeat in the Chino–Japanese War of 1894–1895, it lost Korea, which it had long controlled, and had to cede its island of Taiwan to Japan. The Chinese were shocked that the island "dwarfs," as they called the Japanese, had overwhelmed their great nation with such ease.

Rather late in the day, cries went up at court demanding that China modernize its army, do away with the examination system and the scholar-officials, and open itself up to modern education stressing science and technology.

The reformers, however, were no match for the Dowager Empress Ci Xi, who had been the power behind the throne since 1861, when the last emperor died. Ci Xi was vain, extravagant, wily, conservative, and above all power hungry. She would do anything to keep the reform elements from gaining control, even if this meant the fall of the empire (which it eventually did).

Ci Xi had begun her career as a concubine of the Qing emperor, and at age 16 had born him his first son and heir to the throne. As the child was only five years old when the emperor died, Ci Xi ruled for him as dowager until he was 18. A year after his coronation, the young emperor died under mysterious circumstances. Some said he had died of smallpox, others said of syphilis, and still others whispered of murder. By an odd coincidence, the young emperor's pregnant wife also died a mere three months after he did.

Ci Xi now acted as regent for the new heir, her nephew, who was also a young child. But when he grew up and came to the throne as the leader of the reformers, she moved swiftly to have him removed from power, and put under house arrest until his death in 1908.

During her long reign, Ci Xi divided her time between the Forbidden City, the rich, imperial palace-complex in the heart of Peking, and the lovely lakeside Summer Palace on the city's northwestern fringe. As the old Summer Palace had been looted in 1860 and its greatest treasures sent to Queen Victoria in England and Napoleon III in France, Ci Xi constructed her own splendid cluster of palaces in 1888. She is probably best remembered today for the lavish white marble boat that she ordered built at the edge of the lake. Ci Xi's boat, which of course was never meant to sail, was said to have been paid for out of funds earmarked for the modernization of the imperial navy.

The year 1900 opened the new century on a note of violence. Following China's defeat by the Japanese, hatred of the "foreign devils" reached a fever pitch and was expressed all across north China in a fierce campaign known as the Boxer Rebellion.

The white marble boat at the Summer Palace built by the Dowager Empress Ci Xi.

The Boxers were so named because they had sprung from a secret society called the Society of Righteous and Harmonious Fists. Although weak in weaponry and military skills, its members believed that they were endowed with magical powers that would make them immune to the foreigners' bullets.

Joined by peasants, workers, and soldiers, the Boxers attacked the foreign legations in Peking, killing the high-ranking German and Japanese representatives. They attempted to destroy the foreign-built and owned railways, electric lines, and merchant ships, and to drive the "devils" themselves into the sea. Missionaries and Chinese Christians were also targets of the enraged Boxers, and many were murdered.

The Boxers were doomed to fail, just as the Taiping rebels had been fifty years earlier. Once again the foreign powers, now consisting of the United States and Japan as well as many European nations, sent troops to overcome the rebels. Ci Xi and her court were recalled from exile, where they had retreated during the revolt. More weakened than ever, the Chinese government was forced to pay the foreigners for the lives lost and property damaged. Also, new demands were made for even more foreign control in China.

Finally, in 1905, Ci Xi agreed with her advisers at court that the examination system should be abolished so that Western scientific education could take its place. More than ever, Chinese leaders now felt that the only way to beat the foreigners at their own game was to learn their techniques. Already young Chinese from prosperous families had gone abroad to study, and some, like Dr. Sun Yatsen, were learning more than Western technology. They were learning about democratic forms of government, and also about the rights of nations to govern themselves.

The death of the Dowager Empress Ci Xi in 1908 signaled

the end of the Qing Dynasty. No strong new monarch was on hand to take over for the Manchus. On October 10, 1911, the crumbling old order was swept aside and the nationalist revolutionaries declared that China was from then on a republic.

Sun Yatsen, the first president, had three goals for the new Republic of China. The first was nationalism. This meant that the foreigners were to be driven out of China and the country was to win back its dignity. The second was democracy. The government was to serve the people, and the people, in turn, were to learn to read and write in order to vote and be represented in their government. The third goal was livelihood. China's economic system was to be changed. The peasants would be given land of their own instead of laboring as serfs for the rich landlords. Also, industries would be started to provide new jobs and to modernize the country.

No wonder Sun, as the republic's first president, was called the "George Washington of China." Unfortunately, however, his goals would not be accomplished so easily. China had been ruled by its emperors and scholar-officials for thousands of years. Its people knew nothing about democratic ideas or methods. Most were uneducated, for that had suited the scholar-officials and had kept them powerful. Nor were the rich landowners about to give up their land to the peasants.

The toppling of the empire had been an important move. But it was only the first of many painful steps that would have to be taken to bring about real change. Dr. Sun's China was as misery-ridden as the China of the Manchus had been. Floods, droughts, earthquakes, and other natural disasters still brought widespread famine and death. The strangling of

The Painted Gallery at Ci Xi's Summer Palace, parts of which were destroyed during the Boxer Rebellion.

At the tomb of Dr. Sun Yatsen, the "George Washington of China."

unwanted infants and the selling of wives and children still were common. Bandits continued to roam the countryside, stealing, burning, and raping.

In the cities, the homeless and the sick scavenged for food and died in the streets. And the "blue-eyed barbarians" who had laid claim to China hundreds of years earlier hung on greedily. They were not about to give up their "spheres of influence" in China simply because President Sun Yatsen and his Nationalist Party had declared that they must.

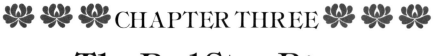

CHAPTER THREE

The Red Star Rises

A visitor to the Republic of China ten years after the fall of the empire would have been horrified. Instead of order, peace, and the beginnings of democracy, the country was in chaos. Most of it was in the hands of petty military chieftains known as warlords. Each warlord had his own army and fought constantly to protect his own small or large domain. Trade and communications had broken down completely. The peasants were at the mercy of ruthless soldiers, and corruption and decay were everywhere.

One of the most powerful warlords of north China, Yuan Shikai, had actually attempted to become emperor and the founder of a new dynasty. But he died in 1916 before realizing this ambition. The only part of China that was still under the control of Dr. Sun Yatsen was the extreme south. There the Nationalist Party, known as the Kuomintang, was headquartered in the city of Canton, a long way from the traditional capital of Peking in the warlord-ravaged north.

Another tragedy befell China at this time. As a result of World War I, which was fought from 1914 to 1918, Germany had lost its foreign concessions in China. However, instead

44

of returning Germany's territory to China, Great Britain, France, and the United States handed it over to their war ally, Japan. This act sparked a fierce protest known as the May Fourth Movement. It began as a student demonstration in Peking on May 4, 1919, and fired up Nationalists throughout the country.

Among the Nationalists, however, there were some who felt that the time had come to take a more radical political approach. Otherwise, China would never be able to drive the foreign imperialists from its soil. One of those who thought along these lines was Mao Zedong, a librarian at Peking University. Mao, like others at the university, was impressed with the 1917 Communist revolution that had recently taken place in Russia. So, on July 1, 1921, he became one of twelve delegates from all over China who met in Shanghai to form the Chinese Communist Party. The Communists believed in the abolition of private property and in a classless society.

Mao had been born in Shaoshan, a village in south China, in 1893. Because, according to Chinese astrology, he had been born in the Year of the Snake and in the Hour of the Green Dragon, it was foretold that he would have a momentous life and that his future would hold bloody and shattering events. At the same time, the Green Dragon in his birth sign represented benevolence and goodness.

Strangely enough, both forecasts came true. Mao, who became China's leader for over fifty years, gave his country both the fiery Red Star that is the symbol of the Communist Party as well as many of the promised benefits of the Green Dragon.

At first, the newly formed Chinese Communist Party hoped to work within the Kuomintang for the liberation and betterment of China. Sun himself, although not a Communist, had become friendly with Communist Russia, now known as the

The young Mao Zedong, one of the founders of the Chinese Communist Party.

Soviet Union. The Soviets seemed willing to help the Chinese against the Western powers, offering them military aid and advice.

Then, in 1925, Sun Yatsen died of cancer while on a visit to Peking. He had gone there hoping to get the warlord who was then in power to cooperate with his government in the south. Chiang Kaishek became the new president.

Chiang had taken part in the 1911 revolution against the Manchus and was believed to share Sun's goals for China. But, as he was strongly anti-Communist in his beliefs, he soon began to take a different course. After a successful opening campaign against the warlords, he suddenly turned on the Communists within the Kuomintang. The Communists had fought loyally in Chiang's army, helping to free

Sun Yatsen's memorial on the slope of the Purple Mountains in Nanjing. Three hundred and ninety-two steps lead to the top.

Nanjing and Shanghai from the grip of the warlords. Yet, in April 1927, Chiang launched a surprise attack on the Communist headquarters in Shanghai. In the reign of terror that followed, hundreds were murdered. Zhou Enlai, who later became one of China's most important Communist leaders, barely managed to escape with his life. Along with Mao and other survivors, he was forced to go into hiding for years.

Chiang now broke all ties with the Soviet Union. He looked to wealthy Chinese landowners and merchants for money to help his armies wipe out the remaining warlords. He also sought backing from the foreign imperialists, promising to keep China free of Communism. The foreign powers accepted Chiang as a responsible leader, and some of the unequal treaties that they had forced the Manchus to sign were even rewritten so that they would be a little more balanced.

However, the old evils still seethed beneath the surface. Land reform was out of the question, for Chiang's government would never ask the wealthy landowners who were supporting him to give up their holdings to the peasants. Poverty, illiteracy, disease, and famine continued to plague the country. Chiang assumed dictatorial powers, introducing strict censorship of the press and building up his secret police force. Taxes were channeled into military defenses against China's enemies—the warlords, who still held on to parts of China; the Communists, who had gone underground; and the Japanese, who in 1931 boldly occupied the region of northeast China known as Manchuria.

The Japanese and the Communists were the two most serious threats to Chiang, with the activities of the Communists the most difficult to track. Mao and his guerrilla forces had gone off into the hilly inland countryside of southern China where, as Mao himself wrote, the Red detachments were "like flowing water and moving clouds." Chiang sent his Kuomintang armies on five separate campaigns against the Communists, but never managed to destroy them.

Mao's strength came from the peasants in the Chinese countryside who had been oppressed for so long by the landlords. Where the Red forces marched, the "local tyrants and evil gentry" were expelled. Sometimes a cruel and corrupt landlord, tax collector, or moneylender was paraded before the people in a tall, pointed, paper dunce cap and mocked by the entire village. As a boy, Mao himself had collected rents for his father who was a small landowner. The peasants had been forced to give up nearly two-thirds of their harvest to the landlord. Most were in debt all their lives. Mao had vowed that this system of human enslavement must be ended.

"A revolution," Mao warned in his early writings, "is not a dinner party." Indeed, the angry peasants sometimes made free with the personal property of the dispossessed landlords. As to the peasants, however, Mao demanded from the start that his guerrilla forces treat them with respect. There was to be no looting, burning, and raping, as were so often done by the armies of the warlords and those of Chiang's Kuomintang. Goods the Red forces confiscated from the landlords were to be brought directly to headquarters. All articles borrowed from the peasants were to be returned. Damaged articles were to be replaced. Food and other items supplied by the peasants were to be paid for at a fair price. The Red soldiers of Mao's People's Liberation Army changed the age-old image of the Chinese soldier as a semi-bandit living off the peasantry.

The ability of the Communists to carve out a domain for themselves in the very heart of Kuomintang China was an infuriating mystery to Chiang Kaishek. In his fifth campaign against the Red "bandits" in 1934, he managed to almost completely surround their territory. Mao, Zhou, and General

Soldiers of new China's People's Liberation Army on a visit to the Great Wall.

Zhu De, the organizer of the Red Army, decided that it was time to escape from Chiang by driving northward and linking up with another Communist guerrilla base at Yanan. This stronghold was located in sandy hill country, amidst craggy mountains, in the great northern loop of the Yellow River.

So began the famous Long March. Joined by many peasants from the south, Mao's forces of over 100,000 started off on a roundabout route on foot, trying to avoid both Chiang's pursuing armies and the ever-hostile soldiers of the warlords. Heading first southwest, then west, and finally north, they covered over 8000 miles, crossing rugged mountains and vast windy plains, swift rivers and sodden marshes.

When, a year later, they reached Yanan, their number had been reduced to only about 20,000. Fewer than 30 were women. Among the many who had lost their lives during the terrible journey was Mao's wife.

At Yanan, however, no longer threatened by Chiang, the Communists established new and permanent strength. Like most of the local peasants, Mao and his people lived in simple cave dwellings dug out of the sandy hillsides. At this head-quarters of China's first Communist government, a large peasant army was trained, schools were established, and the future of China under Mao was planned. No attempts were made at this early stage, however, to attack the Kuomintang.

The next fourteen years brought new and unexpected hardships to the long-suffering Chinese people. Yet, in that period, the way was paved for a Communist victory over the entire country and an end, at last, to foreign domination.

During those years, matters went from bad to worse for the Chiang regime. The Japanese, who had taken Manchuria in 1931 because it was rich in iron and coal, now drove deeper into China's territory. By the beginning of World War II in 1939, Japan occupied most of eastern China, forcing Chiang to move his capital far inland to Chongqing. Even after the United States entered the war in 1941 and began sending aid to Kuomintang China, the Japanese continued to bomb de-fenseless cities and lay waste to the countryside. Much of China's population moved westward into the interior of the country, fleeing the Japanese-occupied cities of Peking, Shanghai, and Canton.

Despite American aid, Chiang did little during the war to halt the Japanese. He actually hoarded the military supplies sent to him, planning to use them against the Communists.

When at last the World War ended with Japan's defeat in 1945, Mao took the offensive against Chiang. He had long planned to claim China for the Communists, who now clashed with the Kuomintang in a civil war.

Even with continued United States' aid, Chiang's regime

was doomed. It was corrupt, inefficient, and cruel. The peasantry feared and hated Chiang's soldiers. Often they rounded up helpless farmers and hurled them into the fight against the Communists. If they were wounded or killed, their emaciated bodies were left to rot where they fell.

Under Chiang's Kuomintang, the economy had failed so badly that the middle classes had begun to desert. The Communists, on the other hand, had won over many of the smaller landowners by allowing them to keep their holdings, provided they treated the peasants fairly.

Through its guerrilla attacks on the Japanese during World War II, the Red Army had improved its skills and increased its supply of weapons. Mao's territory also had expanded, so much so, in fact, that he now controlled about one quarter of China.

The first Communist victory over the Kuomintang after the war was the winning back of Manchuria. Mao's forces then pushed steadily south. Chiang's government was now so weak due to broken morale and the loss of popular support that even the United States gave up trying to help the Kuomintang. In September of 1949, Chiang Kaishek fled to Taiwan with what was left of his government and his army, and with a long-hoarded treasure of many millions of dollars. The large island of Taiwan, about 100 miles off the coast of China, had been liberated from the Japanese at the close of World War II.

In a sense, the Chinese people had made the choice. In supporting the Communists over the Kuomintang, they showed how they felt about Chiang. They resented his loyalty to the rich Chinese and to the foreigners who had preyed on them for so long; they resented his government's indifference to the suffering of the masses.

On October 1, 1949, Mao proclaimed the establishment of

the People's Republic of China in the capital of Peking. After a 22-year struggle against the Kuomintang, the warlords, and the Japanese, the Red Star had risen at last. Or, as Mao declared on viewing a rosy sunrise from the top of the holy mountain of Tai Shan, "the East is Red." As it happens, Tai Shan, which is located near the city of Jinan, is also the legendary home of the benevolent Green Dragon.

The China that Mao inherited upon Liberation lay almost completely in ruins. The Japanese bombings and the war with the Kuomintang had left bridges, dams, railways, and canals in disrepair. Food supplies were so low that the peasant landholders were asked to grow rice and other grains without delay.

On Tiananmen Square in Peking, where Mao proclaimed the People's Republic of China.

Also urgently needed were social changes that would make Mao's China different from that of the dynasties and other forms of government that had come before. New laws were passed at once concerning women's rights, education, and health care.

"Women hold up half the sky." This motto meant that since women in the new society would share responsibilities equally with men, they would also share equally in its benefits. Concubinage, bigamy, child marriage, and other types of forced or arranged marriages were outlawed. Mates were to be chosen freely, and husband and wife were to share equally in family property and in the care of their children. Such practices of the past as killing or selling children became high criminal offenses. If a marriage was not satisfactory, a wife as well as a husband could ask for a divorce.

Foot-binding had been outlawed by Chiang Kaishek's government. But under the Communists it really disappeared, for women's role in society changed drastically. Many women from both rich and poor classes now worked in fields and factories alongside men, became politically active, attended schools and universities, and prepared to enter the professions. Class differences among women broke down as women's opportunities expanded.

Of course, some changes would come about slowly. Country people would cling for a long time to the old custom of the family-arranged marriage. And it would be some years before even small numbers of women would begin to appear in top-ranking posts in industry and government. But at least the old bonds had been broken, and by government decree.

In the China of 1949, 80 percent of the people could neither read nor write. China's ancient literary heritage had been reserved for the scholar-officials and other members of the upper classes. Now Mao launched an all-out campaign

A mother and daughter of new China. Women have been freed of many of the bonds of the past.

for literacy through public schooling for all children and night classes for adults.

Written Chinese, however, with its complicated characters consisting of many strokes, had always been difficult to learn. So the government started a program of simplifying hundreds of characters so they could be written with fewer strokes. Also, to enable all Chinese to understand each other better, the Mandarin dialect of north China was designated the "common speech" of the entire country.

The Cantonese dialect of the south, which is quite different

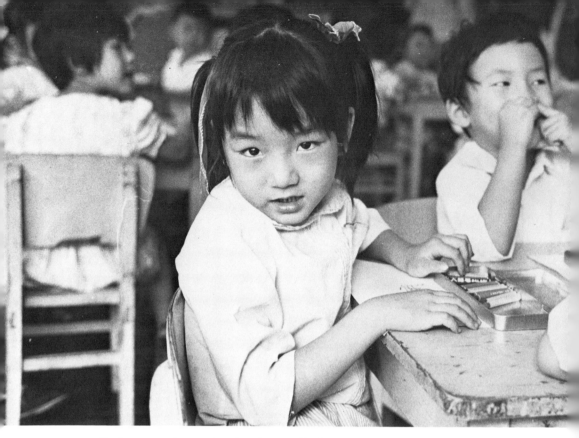

Getting an early start in education—a kindergarten classroom in Shanghai.

from Mandarin, would still be spoken, as would China's many other dialects. However, people would be required to learn Mandarin as well. Fortunately, all of the Han Chinese dialects are written with the same characters.

Mao's campaign to teach the Chinese people to read was so successful that when his famous *Little Red Book* appeared in 1964, millions of copies were distributed and read. This collection of quotations from his writings instructed the army and all the other citizens in discipline and in service to the society.

True, the *Little Red Book* was a propaganda tool. However, the ability to read opened people's minds to other writings as well, like the political wall posters that have appeared in China at various times. These large strips of paper, written

A monument to the armed forces, each figure holding a copy of Mao's
Little Red Book.

and posted by individuals, have contained comments and criticism about working and living conditions and even about the government and the Communist system.

"Away with all pests!" On this note Mao introduced his campaign for health and sanitation in the new China. The "four pests" were flies, rats, bedbugs, and mosquitoes.

China's numerous diseases could be traced directly to a variety of social ills. Syphilis and other venereal diseases probably arrived with the European sailors who made port at Canton in the early 1500's. Drug addiction on a major scale had begun with the first British shipment of Indian-grown opium in 1781. Most of all, poverty and public indifference were to blame for the cholera, plague, smallpox, typhoid, and other epidemics that had killed such large numbers of the Chinese populace in the past.

"Away with all pests!"—a bustling but clean street in modern Wuxi.

Medical care in the countryside—a hospital clinic on a farming commune.

In new China, addictive drugs and prostitution were strictly outlawed, and health care was to be made available to everyone. Doctors and nurses were sent to the countryside. Their methods of treatment combined the best features of Chinese and Western medicine. After a time, "barefoot doctors" were trained. Actually young farmers and other workers in the countryside, they spent part of their time offering health care, doing sanitation work, and teaching others these skills.

The new China, with Mao Zedong as Chairman of the

Communist Party, was not a democracy. People did not have many of the political, civil, and religious rights of the democratic countries of the West. The Communist Party ran China for the people's benefit, as Mao saw it, and no opposition was allowed. Yet for the vast majority of Chinese, hunger, homelessness, disease, illiteracy, and the oppression of women began to vanish quickly as the new system got under way.

By 1956, Mao felt that Communism was succeeding so well in China that people should be allowed some freedom to express their thoughts. Using a quote from the Chinese classics, Mao declared: "Let a hundred flowers bloom together; let a hundred schools of thought contend."

Perhaps Mao really believed that his program would receive nothing but praise; or perhaps he wanted to find out how much hidden opposition there was. The Hundred Flowers Campaign, as it was called, brought an outpouring of criticism against the government, mainly from creative artists and intellectuals. Most of it took the form of "big character" wall posters that appeared in public places where they could be read by everybody. The posters were so called because their Chinese characters had been boldly painted with thick writing brushes.

Mao was horrified that his "hundred flowers" had turned out to be "poisonous weeds." Revolutionary China, for which he had fought so hard, might well be in danger if too many people began to rise in protest. Then what would happen to the new programs that were helping to raise living standards for the mass of the people?

The invitation to speak out politically was abruptly withdrawn. In the Anti-Rightist Campaign of 1957, many of those who had criticized the Communist system were imprisoned, some for long terms.

Meantime, there was much to be done on the economic

front to improve agriculture and develop industry. Already the 100 million small farms that had been taken over by the peasants from the big landowners were being pooled and turned into large farming communes, clusters of group-owned and group-run farming villages. A poor peasant with a bit of land could grow only a little food. But on a commune, with careful planning, better seeds and fertilizer, farm implements and animals to share, and a good irrigation system, the amount of food produced per plot could really increase.

Mao had also begun to bring industry to the countryside in the form of "backyard furnaces" that were to make low-grade steel on the communes. This was one of many steps taken in the Great Leap Forward of 1958, a campaign that Mao declared would help China to "walk on two legs." One leg was agriculture and the other industry.

Droughts, floods, pests, and typhoons took a heavy toll in China during the Great Leap Forward. Although the campaign, which ended in 1960, was not a success, it pointed the way for other kinds of industry to be brought to the countryside. It also proved that regions stricken with famine due to natural disasters need not become wastelands where millions starved. Through good central planning, China's food was rationed and shared so that lives were spared and everyone was adequately fed during the emergency.

As the 1960's advanced, China became remarkably self-sufficient. The country was also very isolated, for the Chinese Communists had almost no friends among the major world powers. The United States, still loyal to Chiang Kaishek on Taiwan, refused to recognize Mao's China. And in 1960 the Russians, who had aided Mao since his victory, suddenly withdrew their friendship. The Chinese–Soviet split was caused by differences of opinion as to how a Communist society should be run.

Mao saw the Soviets as "capitalist roaders." He criticized their "imperialistic" domination of other countries in eastern Europe and elsewhere. He also accused them of having a class system. Party officials, plant managers, scientists, artists, and others formed an elite class in the Soviet Union. They had better salaries, food, clothing, and housing, private automobiles, and foreign-travel privileges.

Mao did not want this "aping of the West" to happen in China. "Persons in authority taking the capitalist road" must be stopped, he declared. When, in 1966, Mao felt that there was too much distance growing between the ordinary Chinese and others in the society, he launched the Cultural Revolution. It was intended to recapture the spirit of equality present at Yanan, when all had struggled together. But it was to be fought with words and deeds—propaganda slogans, massive demonstrations, and examples of personal sacrifice of goods and privileges—instead of guns.

Unfortunately, Mao's well-meant effort to bring back the classless society of the early days of the revolution got badly out of hand. A group of over-eager young people known as the Red Guards came to power. They attacked party officials, university professors, scientists, musicians, artists, writers, and ordinary citizens whom they labeled "class enemies." Many were publicly ridiculed in dunce caps, others were jailed, and some were so cruelly hounded that they were driven to suicide. Thousands were killed. Universities and other schools of higher learning were closed, and both students and teachers were sent to the countryside to help raise pigs, spread manure, and learn the life of the peasantry.

With Premier Zhou Enlai as the guiding force toward moderation, the Cultural Revolution ended officially in 1969. China had lost some of its best thinkers and greatest talents. and the education of its youth had been badly disrupted.

Mao Zedong in his later years, a great but not perfect leader.

Even worse, the evils of the Cultural Revolution lingered on for many more years as Mao's wife, Jiang Qing, and three of her cohorts tried to stifle all efforts at modernization.

Since Mao was now in failing health, Jiang Qing's "Gang of Four" took control of cultural matters. Jiang Qing herself banned all Western music, art, and literature. She even restricted the number of Chinese operas that could be performed to only eight "model revolutionary works."

Mao's death in 1976 brought about the rapid downfall of the Gang of Four. Under the new Communist Party chairman, Jiang Qing and the rest of the Gang were arrested and publicly disgraced. Jiang Qing was given a suspended death sentence. Many Chinese compared her to the last Manchu empress, Ci Xi, in her craftiness and lust for power.

Zhou Enlai, too, died in 1976 and was perhaps more deeply mourned at the time than Mao. He had been widely loved at home and admired abroad. It was largely through his cooperation that the United States and the People's Republic of China had established friendly relations in 1972.

After years of hostility, President Richard M. Nixon's visit to China that year was a historic event. Zhou realized that the American president was offering China friendship because the United States wanted a strong ally against the Soviet Union, and also because it was seeking a vast new commercial market. But as a leader who saw beyond the moment, he realized how useful that friendship would be for China's modernization.

Following the deaths of Zhou and Mao, Deng Xiaoping became China's most important political figure. Although his title was only Vice-Premier, and he had himself been made to wear the dunce cap during the Cultural Revolution, Deng was now given strong support. His goal was to undo the damage of the Cultural Revolution and strive for the "Four

Modernizations"—in agriculture, industry, science and technology, and defense.

The Chinese pendulum had swung once again, away from "shutting the door on the world," as Deng put it, and looking back into the past. But what about Mao, whose body, preserved and lifelike, draped with the red flag of the Chinese Communist Party, lies in state in a crystal sarcophagus in the heart of Peking?

Each day thousands of Chinese and visitors patiently line up before the Mao Zedong Memorial Hall. They enter and

Premier Zhou Enlai welcoming Kurt Waldheim, Secretary-General of the United Nations, to China in 1972.

Vice-Premier Deng Xiaoping (in center) at a Communist Party congress following the death of Mao.

file slowly past his coffin with respect, admiration, and a sense of wonder at his greatness.

"Mao was not perfect," most Chinese will tell you. "Even a great man makes some mistakes." But they know that because of Mao the Red Star rose over China, and thereby the entire world was changed.

CHAPTER FOUR

The Country and the Countryside

China, the land that was locked away from the world for so long, is today receiving more "foreign guests" than ever in its history.

The caravan traders and sea merchants of the early days are now business representatives from all parts of the world. The gunboats of the "blue-eyed barbarians" have been replaced by planeloads of eager tourists from Europe and America. These visitors have been joined by Japanese and other Asians and by "overseas Chinese," the descendants of Chinese emigrants. All want to see and experience the new China.

In the past, China's borders changed with each new dynasty that rose to power. Today its territory is vast, making the People's Republic of China the third largest country in the world, after the Soviet Union and Canada.

What does the Chinese landscape look like? Its terrain, which covers an area of 3.7 million square miles, is enormously varied. But probably China's two most striking features are its rivers and its mountains.

Just as the Great Wall was once the northern boundary of

China, so the Yangtze River is considered the line that divides north and south China. Rising in the high mountains of Tibet, the Yangtze flows eastward for 3100 miles and empties into the East China Sea, which is part of the great Pacific Ocean. Only the Nile and the Amazon are longer than the Yangtze, making China's great river the third longest in the world.

Near the coast of China, the Yangtze is broad and muddy yellow. But inland, as it passes through the famous Yangtze Gorges, it is a narrow, roaring current with dangerous reefs, bends, and shallows that cause foaming rapids and deep whirlpools. The mountains that form the walls of the gorges are so tall and steep that in some places they block out the sun completely, except when it is directly overhead.

Under the new government, the most dangerous passages through the gorges have been blasted and rechanneled to make the river safer for transport. Also, the wider, calmer stretches of the Yangtze have been bridged to make travel between north and south China easier.

The Chinese are especially proud of the Yangtze River Bridge at Nanjing. It was begun in 1960, just as the Russian engineers and advisers were called home to the Soviet Union because of the quarrel between the two nations. The Chinese continued building the bridge on their own. They completed the three-mile-long, two-level span across the deep, silt-filled waters in 1968.

Before the bridge was built, the railway cars of north- and southbound trains had to be disconnected and ferried across the river. This took hours. Now trains, trucks, and buses cross by the bridge in minutes.

"Overseas Chinese" tourists visiting the famous leaning pagoda at Tiger Hill in Suzhou.

The bridge the Chinese proudly built across the Yangtze River at Nanjing.

For the leaders of new China, the linking of the two halves
of China serves as a symbol of the nation's political unity.
This is probably one reason that Mao Zedong chose to swim
across the Yangtze River on July 16, 1964, and again on that
same date in 1966. Although Mao was 73 years old in 1966,
he used this occasion to prove his vigor to the many onlook-
ers and newspaper photographers.

Mao entered the river in the city of Wuhan, where the
distance across is one mile. But as the downstream current
is swift, Mao had to take a diagonal course, covering nearly
eight miles. Thousands of his followers were so inspired by
Mao's example that swimming this route became a yearly
event, repeated every July 16. It was very soon after his his-

toric second swim that Mao started the Cultural Revolution.

Another famous river, the second longest in China, is the Yellow River. Like the Yangtze, it flows from west to east, but farther to the north. China's early civilization grew up along its banks. Because of unexpected changes in its course and frequent devastating floods, the Yellow River has been called China's sorrow. The river takes its name from the yellow soil it carries with it all the way to the Yellow Sea of the Pacific Ocean. Under the Communist government, huge stone dikes have been erected to control flooding. Also, pumping stations have been built to irrigate the surrounding countryside.

The differences between north and south China are quite marked. Dry, windy plains make up much of the north. There is some good farming country in the eastern half, including parts of Manchuria. To the west, however, the land dries out into barren desert.

South of the Yangtze, China is warmer, wetter, and

Terraced farmlands in dry, windy north China. Through great effort, the thin, stony soil has been made fertile.

greener. It also becomes quite hilly as one travels inland from the coast. China's highest mountains are found in the south-western quarter of the country. Most of this region is made up of Tibet, which is today part of China. Mt. Everest, the highest point on Earth, at 29,000 feet, rises on China's border with Nepal in the Himalaya mountain range.

North and south China differ, too, in the foods they grow and eat. The farmers of the northeast raise wheat, corn, and millet. Wheat products like noodles and steamed buns are popular in the north, while the southeast is known as the land of fish and rice. Farmers in the north usually get two crops a year while those in the south get three because of the longer growing season. However, winter greenhouses in new China supply large cities like Peking with fresh vegetables all year round.

Confucius is supposed to have advised the Chinese to eat dishes that were three-quarters vegetables and one-quarter meat. Because meat is costly, most Chinese have followed this rule. They have learned how to cook a delicious variety of fresh vegetables until just crisp and succulent. Also, because foods are cut into small pieces before cooking, they use very little precious cooking fuel in the process.

Pigs, chickens, and ducks are raised almost everywhere in China. The famed Peking ducks, which are force-fed for quick fattening, are the main ingredient of the Peking duck dinner. This type of banquet, containing many courses, is given mainly for officials and visitors. It features chunks of duck meat tucked into little "pocket" buns or rolled up in a thin pancake with scallions and a sweet-spicy bean sauce. Other parts of the duck also appear at the dinner, ranging from the liver to the webbing between the toes. As a result of their long experience with famine when people ate even tree bark to try to stay alive, the Chinese have learned never to throw away anything that is edible.

Therefore, many animal parts and all sorts of sea creatures that are unfamiliar foods to many Westerners appear in Chinese dishes. They include the squid and the octopus with their waving tentacles, the jellyfish, and the fat, wormlike sea cucumber, or sea slug.

In Inner Mongolia, north of the Great Wall, there is so little rainfall that most of the land is too dry for farming, and animal herding is still the main occupation. Possibly one of the reasons the Han Chinese seldom drank milk or ate cheese was because they looked down upon their "barbarian" Mongol enemies who did.

Down through the centuries, the Han Chinese's substitute for dairy products was the soybean, which is high in protein and can be made into a "soy cheese." Even today milk is sold mainly for children or invalids in Han China, although most people have come to like ice cream.

Still drier than Inner Mongolia is Xinjiang to the extreme northwest, a land of bitterly cold winters and burning hot summers. The Turpan Depression, a green oasis and the lowest point in China at 505 feet below sea level, is located here. In the early days the Turpan oasis was a gathering place for caravans traveling between China and the Middle East along the old Silk Road.

Melting snows running down from the mountain chains that rim parts of the desert make it possible to grow some grains and a little fruit. However, the Uygur and Kazakh people of Xinjiang are mainly nomadic sheepherders.

Unlike the Mongols, the Uygurs and Kazakhs are not Oriental looking. They are related to the Turks and look more like Europeans. As they are Muslims, they are forbidden by their religion to eat pork because pigs are considered to be unclean. Shashlik, chunks of lamb threaded onto a sword or skewer and cooked over an open fire, is one of their special dishes.

Another large region inside the borders of China inhabited by a non-Han people is Tibet. The Tibetans follow a religion called Lamaism that springs from Buddhism. For centuries they were ruled by an all-powerful high priest known as the Dalai Lama. During the Yuan Dynasty, in the thirteenth century, the Mongols invaded Tibet and were converted to its religion. As a result, many of the people of Inner Mongolia are also Lama Buddhists.

Under the Manchus, in 1720, China claimed to have conquered Tibet. But its control of this deeply religious and fiercely independent mountain people was very weak. In fact, an Indian traveler of the 1800's who visited Tibet disguised as a lama monk told how he had seen a Chinese beheaded because he had appeared illegally in the holy city of Lhasa.

The Chinese were content to let this snowy, windswept "roof of the world" act as a buffer between China and India until World War II proved that modern aircraft could soar over the forbidding mountains. So, in 1950, Mao annexed Tibet to the People's Republic of China. The Tibetans strongly opposed the annexation, and there are still pockets of resistance to Chinese rule.

As in the case of the Mongols and the Uygurs, the Tibetan way of life is very different from that of the Han Chinese. Barley is the main cereal crop, and the long-haired yak provides meat, milk, cheese, and butter. Along with the Mongolians, the Tibetans like to put lumps of butter into their steaming cups of tea.

Two other large groups of minority people are the Muslim Hui of the Ningxia region on the border with Outer Mongolia and the Zhuang, also Muslims, who live in Guangxi near the border with Vietnam. Altogether there are 55 different minority groups inside China, totaling about 6 percent of the entire population. Although the percentage seems small,

In the high Himalayas, looking toward Mt. Everest on the border between Tibet and Nepal.

China has about 1 billion people. So its minorities alone number 60 million. Like the Tibetans, other minority groups resisted Chinese Communist rule. To ease relationships, the government has granted them special privileges.

In the People's Republic of China, the areas where the five largest minorities live are called autonomous regions. This means that the local people may wear their own dress, speak their own language, have their own schools, and follow their own religions.

At the same time, most of the autonomous regions border on countries with which China is not on very friendly terms, like the Soviet Union, India, and Soviet-influenced Outer Mongolia. So many Han Chinese troops, officials, and specialists have been sent to the autonomous regions to secure the borders, introduce the Communist system, and develop agriculture and industry.

Inner Mongolia, for example, now has communes for animal raising, more farming than in the past, mining, and even an iron-and-steel industry. Xinjiang and Tibet are not yet quite as developed, but they do have new hospitals, schools, and public works. Children in all the minority areas now learn Mandarin as well as their local language.

China's minorities live on about 50 percent of its land, most of it consisting of mountains, plains, and deserts. Before Liberation, non-Han peoples were looked down upon as "barbarians." Today, though, new China is being educated to appreciate the value of its minority peoples, not only for political and military reasons, but for their productivity as farmers, herders, and factory workers.

The traditions of the national minorities are being recognized, too. Muslim mosques and Tibetan temples that were closed during the Cultural Revolution have now been reopened. And troupes of costumed dancers and singers from the minority areas tour the country so that all Chinese can enjoy their rich and colorful performances.

Aside from its five autonomous regions, the People's Republic of China is divided into 22 provinces and three municipalities. The municipalities consist of China's three largest cities—Shanghai, Peking, and Tianjin—and their immediate surroundings.

If the new government has redrawn the map of China, it has also changed the face of the countryside. Although China is a very big country, only about 12 percent of it is really good farmland. To reclaim as much land as possible and to im-

Han Chinese schoolchildren performing dances in the styles of the national minorities.

prove the fertility of the soil, dams, canals, and other irrigation projects have been built. In level country, the irrigation ditches run straight as rulers between the fields. On hilly land, swirling terraces of earth edged with stone embankments make the steep slopes fertile. Millions of trees have also been planted to prevent erosion, serve as windbreaks, and renew forests.

Wherever it is farmed, the Chinese countryside looks like a patchwork quilt in dozens of shades of green, each leaf and blade carefully tended. In addition to rice—the greenest of all patches—the crops may be tea, cotton, bamboo, barley, wheat, sweet potatoes, beans, cabbage, onion, garlic, eggplant, turnips, cucumbers, and numerous other vegetables.

As China was always a peasant society, it is not surprising that 80 percent of its population—about 800 million people —live in the countryside, most of them working as farmers. Even today, very little machinery is used on Chinese farms. Laborsaving farm machines would lead to unemployment for farm workers who would then look for jobs in the already overcrowded cities. Even now, Chinese who want to move from the countryside to the cities must get official permission.

One answer to the problem of China's large and growing farm population has been to bring some industry to the farming communes. Today there are over 60,000 communes. Most can be compared to small or medium-size towns. Although their main business is growing the food that China needs to feed its one billion people, communes may also have small factories that make machine parts or pesticides, mill flour, or can fruits and vegetables. All communes have repair shops for farm implements and vehicles. Many have fish hatcheries and some raise oysters for cultured pearls. At communes outside the silk-manufacturing cities of the

Yangtze plain, silkworms are raised for the silk mills of Wuxi, Hangzhou, and Suzhou.

On the communes, the tiny black worms are set out on large straw trays to feed on mulberry leaves until they grow large and white and begin to spin their cocoons. The fluffy cocoons are then sent to the silk-reeling factories in town where they are sorted and soaked so that each will unwind in a single long silken thread. The threads of several cocoons are twisted together for strength, and the silk is then wound onto reels for weaving into silk cloth.

Life on a commune is run along the same lines as in the farming villages of China before Liberation. People live in their own houses and go off to work in the fields each day. But now the work is organized through production brigades made up of many smaller production teams, so that plans can be carried out efficiently. Each farm worker on the commune is paid according to the number of work points he or she contributes. Work points are based on the number of hours spent on a particular job, like planting crops, harvesting, caring for the pigs or other animals, and so forth.

As in the past, the farmers own their own houses. Instead of having mud walls, though, the newer ones are built of brick. Commune families usually can save enough money to improve their houses; but if not, a loan may be available from the production brigade. Upkeep costs very little. Electricity is cheap, and families in the north are kept warm in winter by the old-fashioned *kang*. A *kang* is a large shelf or platform made of earth, big enough for a whole family to sleep on. It is warmed by a fireplace beneath it that can also be used for cooking.

Most commune houses do not have indoor toilets. Throughout history, the Chinese have used human as well as animal wastes to fertilize their fields. Even though China now

produces chemical fertilizers, human wastes, known as night soil, are made good use of. On the communes, the contents of the family's outdoor pit toilet are regularly collected into "honey buckets" or "honey carts" and taken to sealed storage tanks where they are allowed to ferment for several weeks or months. The odors and harmful bacteria disappear and the fertilizer that results is used to enrich the growing crops.

Under the commune system, farmers can no longer own the land they work. But each family is allowed to have a patch of land on which to grow its own vegetables and fruit, raise chickens, ducks, and even a pig or two for private use or to sell at the "free market" in town.

During the Cultural Revolution, these rights were taken away as being "capitalistic," and it was found that production on the commune-held farmlands actually dropped. Farm families like having the chance to earn a little extra money selling eggs, chickens, and vegetables. In winter, when there is less outdoor work, many make handicrafts of straw and bamboo, children's toys, and articles of clothing to sell in town.

At the markets, city and country people get a chance to mingle, and city people often find a more interesting variety of things to buy than at the regular stores.

The Chinese communes also have been successful because members get a chance to vote on local matters and to take part in the planning. Now the wealth is divided much more evenly than when the rich landlords held most of the land, and the farmers have a higher standard of living. Many own

(Above) Sorting silkworm cocoons that have come from the communes, at a silk-reeling factory in Wuxi.
(Below) Silk threads spun from the cocoons being wound onto reels for weaving into cloth.

Farmers from a commune who have come to town to sell apples grown on their private plots of land.

bicycles, sewing machines, radios, watches, and new furniture and household utensils.

The communes provide health clinics, hospitals, schools, and recreation. Movies and live entertainment by acrobatic, dance, and puppetry troupes may provide leisure-time activities. In summer, performances may be given on a stage put up in an open field, with each person bringing a stool to sit on.

Of course, farm life in China still consists of very hard work and is often extremely monotonous. Young people who want to develop special talents, attend schools of higher learning, or just travel to other parts of the country may find it very constricting. For this reason, many young men and women from the countryside choose to join the armed forces.

Because of China's huge population, there are so many applicants for military service that the country does not need to have a draft. In other words, it is not compulsory in China to serve in the armed forces. In fact, only about one person out of every ten who apply is enlisted in China's People's Liberation Army, which numbers about four million.

Enlistees must be between 18 and 32 years old. They serve for either three years in the army, four in the navy, or five in the air force. Members of the armed forces get all their food and clothing, plus spending money each month. In addition, their families on the communes get extra points for having a son or daughter in the service.

The motto of the armed forces is "Serve the people." Their number-one job, of course, is to protect the country. However, members of the military may also help out with road building or farming projects or take part in scientific experiments. In addition, they assist the public during emergencies and disasters. During the Cultural Revolution, when the Red Guards went on a rampage, it was the army that was called in to restore order.

All enlistees get political training so they can better understand the duties and rewards of the Communist system. Women in the services get less military training than men. Many work in military hospitals and on army posts. Off duty, China's officers and enlistees mingle freely with the people. The uniform of the army is green, the navy blue, and members of the air force wear a green jacket and blue trousers. In keeping with Mao's own example at Yanan, uniforms have no special insignia showing rank. The only way to tell an officer from an enlistee is by the number of pockets on the jacket. An enlistee has two pockets, while an officer has four.

(Above) Young army enlistees from all over China being given a tour of the Nanjing Museum. (Left) Off-duty army officers taking photographs in the rain at a garden in Hangzhou. Only the number of pockets on their uniform jackets indicate their rank.

After a stint in China's armed forces, most of the enlistees return to civilian life. Many have learned useful new skills that can be applied in the countryside. They also have had the chance to visit parts of China they might otherwise never have seen.

Once these young people have returned to civilian life, their next step probably is marriage and raising a family. The government, however, hopes that this will not happen too soon and that couples will have only one child, or perhaps two at the very most.

With one billion people, China already has one-fourth of all the people on Earth. Even with improvements to make farmlands more fertile, it has only a limited amount of land for growing food. Cities and industrial belts are expanding onto this land, too. Therefore, if China is to continue feeding all its people, the birth rate must be kept very low.

Studies have shown that women nearer to the age of 30

tend to have fewer children. So the Chinese government tries to persuade couples not to marry before the woman is at least 25 and the man 28.

A family with only one child receives special privileges. The mother may be given a whole year off from work to care for the baby and may be paid 80 percent of her salary. The family will have extra ration coupons for certain foods or other items that may be in short supply. Also, the child will have opportunities to attend special schools. If a second child is born, however, many of these privileges will be lost for the entire family. Parents who want to have a third child will be urged not to by members of their courtyard or neighborhood committee.

Because apartments are so cramped and most mothers work away from home, city people are more likely to have

A sister and brother from a farm family on a commune outside Wuxi.

A child growing up in the countryside of new China.

only one child than families in the countryside. Nevertheless, all over China, families are much smaller than they used to be. People tend to put the good of the entire country above their individual desires.

The children who are born to Chinese families nowadays are loved and cared for, healthy and well dressed, treasured but not spoiled. Gone are the ragged, hungry children of the past, with bloated bellies and sticklike arms and legs, the diseased, the crippled, and the homeless. Gone also is the need to drown or strangle the newborn, or to sell young children into slavery or prostitution.

Whether they live in the cities or the countryside, the children of new China are growing up with a feeling of pride in their country, hope for the future, and most of all, a sense of responsibility to all around them.

CHAPTER FIVE

The Cities of New China

China's cities have changed even more than its countryside since the Red Star rose over the nation in 1949. Before Liberation, city sidewalks teemed with human misery. Starving families begged for food, exhausted coolies dropped in their tracks, and each morning dead bodies had to be removed from the streets. Filth and evil smells, rats and insects were everywhere.

Today, China's cities are more crowded than ever. Peking, with nine million people, is larger than New York City. Shanghai, with over 11 million, is the largest city in China and also one of the largest in the world. Yet life in the cities is very different from what it was in the past. Streets are free of dirt and litter. Everyone appears clean, healthy, properly fed, and neatly dressed. People go about their business calmly and purposefully.

China's cities are surprisingly quiet, too. This is because most people travel by bicycle in a never-ending stream, often riding ten or twelve bikes abreast. No one is permitted to own a private automobile in new China. The cars one does see belong to the government and are used for official business.

A traffic-police booth on a street corner in modern Shanghai.

Trucks and buses cause most of the traffic noise that is heard. Drivers beep steadily at the bikers who ride too close or daringly try to cross their paths. But on the wider streets dividers have been built to provide safe traffic lanes for the bicyclists.

City parking lots are an amazing sight with their rank upon rank of bicycles. Outsiders cannot help wondering how a Chinese factory worker or department-store shopper finds his or her bike in these forests of wheels and handlebars. Peking alone has three million bicycles, and all riders in the capital must have a permit.

Buses are another convenient way of getting around in big cities. In Peking, fares depend on how far one is going. A trip of about two miles costs only 5 fen, or 3 cents. Peking and Shanghai also have subway systems that are clean, quiet, speedy, and equally cheap.

However, not every trace of old China has disappeared when it comes to transport. Goods and sometimes passengers are carried through the streets in three-wheeled pedicabs that are foot pedaled, like tricycles, by their drivers. Heavy loads are often transported in two-wheeled carts that are pushed or pulled. And many Chinese still use the bamboo shoulder pole. Laden baskets, buckets, or other burdens are hung from the ends of the pole to balance it.

Suitcases and bundles are often carried this way by travelers at railway stations. Just before boarding the train, the passenger detaches the baggage from the ends of the shoulder pole. Then all three items are neatly stowed away on the luggage racks of the railway car for the duration of the trip.

Visitors are always impressed with the uniformity of dress

Bicycles parked outside the well-stocked No. 1 Department Store in Wuxi.

The ancient Chinese shoulder pole, still used to transport burdens on city streets and in the countryside.

that is especially noticeable in Chinese cities. In summer, it seems that almost all men and women wear white shirts or blouses over blue, gray, or green trousers. In cooler weather, the blue or gray high-collared, buttoned jackets known as Mao jackets appear.

Actually these should be called Sun jackets, for they really are modeled on the dress of Dr. Sun Yatsen, first president of the Chinese republic. Mao and his followers adopted this jacket as being most practical for men and women. Even China's leaders do not appear in neckties and business suits. This type of dress is still too strongly associated with the foreigners of the West and the bourgeoisie, or property-owning classes.

Dressing alike is not a practice that resulted from China's Communist revolution, however. Throughout their long history, the Han Chinese as well as the minority peoples on their borders followed a traditional style of standard dress. Only the very wealthy could indulge in individually styled garments.

Yet it is certainly wrong to label today's Chinese an "army

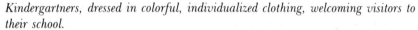

Kindergartners, dressed in colorful, individualized clothing, welcoming visitors to their school.

of blue ants," as some Westerners have done. Children are lovingly outfitted in bright colors and patterns, even ruffles and bows. Schoolgirls in Shanghai have begun to appear in velvet skirts in deep, rich hues. Yard goods in prints and solid colors are offered for sale in the shops. Many Chinese have sewing machines at home for turning these fabrics into garments for young and old.

Housing in Chinese cities ranges from cramped, single-story courtyard houses to new, high-rise buildings. In Peking there are still many old-fashioned courtyard dwellings. The blocks of hutlike quarters have blank, mud-colored walls facing to the outside. A narrow alleyway leads to the central courtyard, onto which all the house doors open.

Just as in the countryside, China's older city dwellings have no running water or indoor flush toilets. Here, too, human wastes are collected from outdoor courtyard toilets and other public latrines to be treated and used as farm fertilizer.

One reason for the many older "flat houses" and other squat structures found in Peking is that during the days of the empire no building could be taller than the palaces of the Forbidden City where the imperial rulers lived. Today, however, Peking is changing rapidly. The city looks like a vast construction site, as housing, offices, hotels, and other high-rise buildings are erected to take care of its growing population.

In Shanghai, China's largest city, the government has made a strong effort to relieve inner-city crowding. On the city's outskirts, it has built hundreds of four- and five-story apartment buildings known as "worker's residential areas." Most of the residents are employed in nearby factories and industrial plants. Each of the residential areas is a miniature town with tens of thousands of inhabitants. Each has its own stores, parks, library, post office, movie theater, nurseries, kindergartens, schools, health stations, and small hospital.

Old houses along China's canals, built of bricks, clay, and tiles.

Buildings in a workers' residential area on the outskirts of Shanghai.

A typical apartment for a family of four or five that includes one or two retired grandparents consists of two rooms and a small kitchen and bathroom. Each room is neatly arranged with a couch that doubles as a bed, a table, and a bureau. Chinese families have always lived close together in snug quarters. The addition of a simple kitchen and bathroom, which do not have to be shared with neighbors, is a real luxury.

Residents planting a garden on a small patch of ground in front of their housing block.

Rents are very low, only about 12 yuan, or seven dollars a month. As the average factory worker earns about 70 yuan a month, a family with two members working has 140 yuan. So the family spends less than 10 percent of its total income for rent.

Retired workers, like the grandparents who live with the family, have a pension for life of 70 to 80 percent of their salaries, and they get free medical care and other benefits. To make way for the numerous young people who enter the work force each year, men retire at age 60 in new China and women at age 50 if they are factory workers, or 55 if they hold clerical or professional jobs.

If men and women are supposed to be equal, why is there a difference in their retirement ages? The government explains that women are retired earlier to make up for their long years of mistreatment before Liberation. Now that the average life span in China is 68 for men and 70 for women, women especially have many years to enjoy a comfortable retirement. Before Liberation, the average person lived only to the age of 32.

Chinese grandparents who live with a family in which both parents work are able to take care of their grandchild or grandchildren. But their usefulness goes beyond the immediate family. Many are members of "residents' committees," on which they serve without pay. The committees help run neighborhood nurseries and kindergartens, have political discussion groups, and try to keep the life of the community orderly and peaceful. The residents' committees are responsible to larger, more formal units called neighborhood committees.

The first neighborhood committees were formed soon after Liberation. They carried on sanitation campaigns to clean up the cities, did welfare work among the sick and the

Grandparents who live with the family care for young children while parents are at work.

poor, and organized literacy classes. Nowadays they act mainly as a link between the individual city dweller and the local government in such official matters as getting ration coupons, housing permits, and marriage licenses.

There is no question that life in new China is closely regulated. Even family matters come to public attention. If a man is mistreating his wife or a family is having a third or fourth child, if young people are behaving dishonestly or immodestly, members of the residents' committee in their housing unit will speak to them and try to engage them in "corrective" group discussions. They will point out that abusing women, increasing China's birth rate, stealing, or behaving immorally are crimes against society and, therefore, political crimes.

Although Communism rules Chinese life, only about 5 percent of China's huge population actually holds membership in the Communist Party. Everyone over 18 is eligible to join the Party, but only those who have been politically active from youth have a really good chance to be considered. Active young people might be drawn from an organization like the Young Pioneers, who are easily identified by the red ties they wear. To become members of this group, schoolchildren must be chosen by their teachers and fellow students as models of good revolutionary behavior and political promise. Young Pioneers instruct others on the importance of the class struggle and take part in ceremonies honoring China's revolutionary heroes.

Most Chinese, however, have little to say in their government. They can vote only for party-approved candidates in local elections and for party-approved members of the peo-

A Shanghai schoolgirl wearing the red tie of the Young Pioneers.

ple's congresses, not for the nation's leaders who have the greatest political power. Yet most people seem to care deeply about the well-being of their country and are willing to cooperate for the public good.

Every day is a work day in China. There is no Sunday or other Sabbath holiday. Factories, stores, and other businesses operate for seven days. But each worker does get one day off a week, and family members try to arrange to be free on the same day.

Most city dwellers work in factories. Some do skilled jobs in China's traditional arts and crafts like ivory and jade carving, embroidery, fan painting, and porcelain making. To learn these specialized jobs, young people must be trained and often have to serve three years as an apprentice. Carpet weaving and the reeling and weaving of silk are other industries that existed in China long before Liberation and are still being carried on today. Most of China's arts and crafts products are made for export.

Today China has a large iron-and-steel industry, as well as its own oil fields, oil refineries, and petrochemical plants. It makes its own cars, trucks, tractors, elevators, electrical equipment, electronics parts, and machinery. For its millions of consumers, China manufactures watches, cameras, sewing machines, bicycles, electric fans, and television sets. TV sets are still rather expensive, so most people watch on publicly owned sets on their farming communes or in neighborhood community centers. A black-and-white set costs about two hundred dollars and a color set about six hundred dollars.

Although China has less air pollution from automobile exhaust than most other countries, there is a great deal of industrial pollution. Many of China's big industrial factories were started with Soviet help in the 1950's and were not very carefully designed. Dense smoke belching from factory chim-

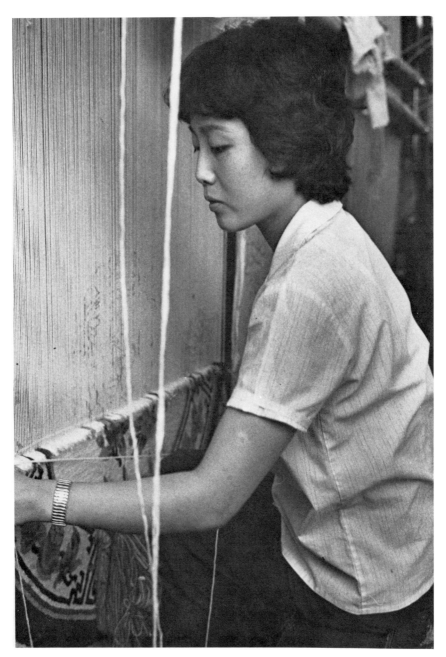
A skilled worker in China's carpet-weaving industry.

neys often hangs over some of China's cities, mingling with the heavy dust particles that blow southward from the deserts and dry plains of Inner Mongolia.

Some Chinese, especially street sweepers, wear gauze masks to filter out the pollutants. Also, the government has planted a great many avenues of trees in the cities. They provide shade and beauty, and partially reduce the bad effects of industrial pollution. In Nanjing alone, 34 million trees have been planted since Liberation, ten for each of its 3.4 million residents.

Just as China's commune dwellers are allowed to have private farming plots, China's city dwellers are permitted to run small individual businesses as street vendors, barbers, cobblers, tailors, or service or repair people. Some families have even opened small noodle or dumpling shops or other types of simple restaurants. However, no privately run business is allowed to have employees from whose labor the owner would profit, as this would be considered a form of capitalism.

The growth of modern industry in China since Liberation has sharpened the differences between its city and country population. Life may be crowded in the cities, but city people have more money and there are more things to buy. Also there are provisions for child care and many more opportunities for education, enrichment, and self-improvement.

In the cities, a working mother may be able to take her child along to the factory where she works and leave it at the plant's day nursery or kindergarten. The child will be fed and cared for throughout the working day. The fathers of new China's small families also tend to help out more with household chores. So, often whichever parent gets home first will prepare the evening meal. And during their free time, many fathers take over the care of the baby or small child. In the

A Chinese father wheeling a typical homemade baby buggy on Tiananmen Square in Peking.

countryside, by contrast, there are usually many more family members and neighbors to care for the children of working parents.

School begins at age seven. But as the Chinese figure age from the time of conception rather than the time of birth, the child is really only six, according to Western calculations, when it begins elementary school. After six years, children go on to the middle schools. Most children in the countryside do not get beyond the three years of junior middle school, so their formal education ends when they are 16.

In the cities, almost all young people complete the three additional years of senior middle school, or high school. They then enter the work force or perhaps attend a technical school for special training.

Getting into a university is quite a feat, as there are not enough places. Entrance exams are so difficult that only one out of every twenty-five high-school graduates goes on to college. University students do not have to pay for their tuition or living quarters, and they receive a small sum of money from the government each month to help with their expenses.

Young people who live in the cities are not only more likely to get into the universities than those who live in the countryside. They also have the chance to attend the "children's palaces." The first of many children's palaces in new China was opened in Shanghai after Liberation. It was housed in a mansion that once belonged to a wealthy foreign family.

Schoolchildren from the elementary grades through high school go to the palaces on a part-time schedule to enrich their skills and creative talents. They study music, dance, acting, painting, model building, and other subjects. They are chosen by their schools and may attend for a number of months or for years. Often their teachers are professionals who are masters in their fields. This path to special achievement is not open to children who live on the communes far from China's major cities, where the palaces are located.

Health care is generally better, too, in the cities. Even though Mao made a special effort to improve health in the countryside through his campaign to train "barefoot doctors," most doctors have remained in the cities, and the best hospitals are there.

City neighborhoods also have many "worker doctors" who staff local health stations and factory clinics. Like the "barefoot doctors," they are paramedics who have been trained by professionals. They have taken over the jobs of giving inoculations, teaching about birth control, and treating common ailments and everyday injuries. About half of the "worker doctors" are women.

Ever since Liberation, both Western and Chinese medicine have been practiced in China. In the traditional Chinese treatment of illness, herbal remedies and acupuncture are widely used. In acupuncture, very fine needles that may be as long as 10 inches are inserted into the body at special points and are sometimes twirled. The needles do not cause pain, only perhaps a slight tingling sensation. Acupuncture treatment is said to relieve headaches, arthritis, rheumatism, and similar ailments. The Chinese have also found that needles inserted at certain points near the ear can restore some hearing, especially for those who have become deaf as a result of a childhood disease.

Acupuncture works in an even more astonishing way. In Chinese hospitals, many types of operations on the heart, abdomen, neck, and other parts of the body can be performed on patients who are anesthetized by acupuncture. The patient remains completely awake and even speaks to the doctors during the surgery. Only the part being operated on is numbed.

Often the needles are twirled by electric current to deepen and prolong the anesthesia. The Chinese also use chemical anesthesia, like that used in the West, in certain cases. But they find that patients who have had acupuncture anesthesia recover much more quickly with no bad aftereffects.

Most Chinese who are government workers in the cities or members of farming communes are covered for all medical

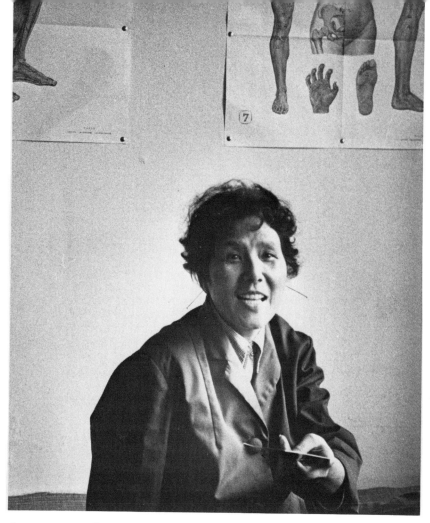

Acupuncture needles inserted behind both ears to treat deafness. Charts above show acupuncture points on the human body.

expenses through their jobs. For those who are not fully covered, costs are very low. An operation to remove an appendix or repair a hernia would be about 8 yuan, or five dollars. A delicate brain operation would be the most expensive, about 30 yuan, or eighteen dollars.

Since China has become industrialized, there has been a rise in on-the-job accidents in factories. Chinese surgeons have shown extreme skill in rejoining arms, hands, feet, and even toes and fingers cut off by high-powered machinery. In fact, China's doctors are among the best in the world in microsurgery.

Today, the main causes of death in China are heart attacks, cancer, and construction accidents. The first two can probably be linked to widespread cigarette smoking and industrial pollution, and also to the fact that people are living longer and so die of the more slowly developing diseases. But on the whole, China's death rate is far lower than in the days before Liberation, when epidemics, starvation, and natural disasters carried off so many.

White is the color of mourning in China, while red is for weddings and other celebrations. Because there is so little space for the living in that crowded country, the dead are usually cremated rather than buried. Mao, entombed in his memorial mausoleum on Tiananmen Square in Peking, is an exception. But Zhou Enlai, China's other great leader, instructed that his body should be cremated like that of most Chinese. His ashes were then scattered over the land from an airplane as a symbol of his belonging to all China.

In China's cities, every day appears to be a holiday because so many workers are having their weekly day off. As houses and apartments are cramped and crowded, people look for recreation away from home for the day. They visit gardens, parks, zoos, palaces, museums, and royal tombs. Most were once private preserves, but they now are open to all. Many people take boat rides on the lakes and rivers, or go on bus or train outings to the Great Wall, the Ming Tombs, or other famous sites.

Temples and pagodas as well as grottoes and caves carved with figures of the Buddha draw many Chinese. However, except for the elderly, most people do not visit these places for religious reasons. They are there as sightseers. While the Chinese government does not at all encourage religious ob-

servance for its citizens, it does help maintain many religious buildings because of their beauty and historical importance.

Officially there are no religious holidays in new China. The main government holidays are New Year's Day on January 1, May Day on May 1, and the two-day National Day holiday on October 1 and 2, the anniversary of Liberation. May Day (which honors the working classes and is celebrated in many other countries as well) and the National Days are marked by great parades.

There is also a three-day official holiday for the Spring Festival, which is also known as Chinese New Year. As this ancient festival follows the moon calendar, it falls at a different time each year, usually in late January or early February. Many workers do not get any other vacation, so this three-day holiday is a favorite time for visiting relatives who live some distance away.

Chinese New Year is brilliantly and noisily celebrated with rockets, sizzlers, and other fireworks that are supposed to drive away evil spirits. But during the Cultural Revolution such celebrations were frowned upon as being "old superstitions." The "Anti Four-Olds" Campaign of the Cultural Revolution tried to do away with old ideas, old superstitions, old customs, and old life-styles.

Another holiday that most Chinese still observe, though it is not an official holiday, is the autumn full-moon festival in September. Delicious thick, round moon cakes stuffed with crystallized fruits, nuts, and sweetened bean paste are sold everywhere. Each city and region has its own variation of these mouth-watering treats. Moon cakes, too, were banned during the Cultural Revolution, as they were considered to be among the "Four Olds."

A Buddhist temple grotto in Hangzhou that attracts more Chinese sightseers than worshippers.

Also frowned upon were card playing and Chinese chess playing, favorite pastimes that are once again openly popular. There are many other games that Chinese enjoy. Children play hopscotch, marbles, and jump-rope. Favorite sports are basketball, volleyball, gymnastics, swimming, and, of course, Ping-Pong. It was at Mao's invitation that a United States Ping-Pong team visited the People's Republic for the first time in 1971, one year before President Nixon's visit reunited the two countries in friendship.

In the early morning hours in streets, parks, and court-

Playing games of chance, a favorite Chinese pastime.

yards, the Chinese may be seen practicing a very ancient form of body movement and mind relaxation known as Tai Ji Quan. Gentle twisting, bending, turning, and stretching exercises are slowly and gracefully coordinated. In factories, too, workers will often use their break time to run through some of the smooth, balanced movements of one of the many Tai Ji exercises. Often they look as though they are moving puffs of cloud about or reaching in slow motion for the tail of a bird.

The Chinese are great movie fans. They enjoy old Charlie Chaplin films and musicals from America like "The Sound of Music." Selected films from other countries are also shown, and there is a growing Chinese movie industry.

Theaters are also packed for Chinese stage entertainments. Some, like the Chinese opera, have roots going back hundreds of years. The famous Peking opera is but one of many local and regional forms of these glittering spectacles. The characters wear exquisite costumes and makeup. With song, music, pantomime, and dance they play out a complicated story, which may take four hours or more. Coming from their drab homes and workaday lives, the Chinese audiences are dazzled by the theatrical richness and also tend to comment on the action throughout the performance.

Since the fall of the Gang of Four, a new form of entertainment is an evening of Western popular music played by Chinese musicians who have mastered Western instruments. Female singers dressed in glamorous Western-style gowns and male singers in Western-tailored suits sing ballads and love songs that are international favorites. Such performances would have been unthinkable during the Cultural Revolution when all forms of art and entertainment had to have a revolutionary theme.

American music has been a special favorite of the Chinese

ever since the Nixon visit of 1972 when songs like "Oh, Susanna" and "Home on the Range" were first played in new China. For several years following, the influence of the Gang of Four kept this music at bay. But today Chinese groups can be heard on tapes and "live," playing "Red River Valley," "Beer-Barrel Polka," "Yankee Doodle," and even some American rock music.

The influence of the West is strong in China and growing steadily. Westernizing seems to go hand in hand with the drive for the Four Modernizations, which depend largely on the import of foreign technology. Japan, with its Western economy, is now China's biggest trading partner. Trade with the United States has expanded greatly, too.

On streets, in railway stations, and in other public places in China political propaganda has given way to commercial advertising. During the Cultural Revolution, people wore Mao buttons on their jackets. Pictures and statues of Mao were everywhere, and billboards urged people to "Never Forget the Class Struggle." Today there are far fewer public images of Mao, and billboards that once carried political slogans now advertise tape recorders, radios, toothpaste, cameras, and other commercial products.

Yet China is far from becoming a mirror of the West. In spite of its modern industries and new consumer goods, much of the country still runs on human labor that is often very close to drudgery. And politically China is still a restricted society, as proven by the "Democracy Wall" episode of the late 1970's.

Between the fall of 1978 and the spring of 1979, the Chinese government permitted its people a brief opportunity for

Drawing household water from a street spigot beneath a billboard advertising commercial products.

"open discussion" in the form of "big character" posters. Best known were those that appeared on the so-called Democracy Wall in Peking. Many of those who wrote posters told of the horrors and cruelties of the Cultural Revolution. Some openly blamed Mao for the Gang of Four and even suggested that he was their fifth member. They rated the dead leader as having been only 70 percent right and 30 percent wrong.

The new government of Vice-Premier Deng Xiaoping might have allowed this airing of grievances against past injustices. But some of the posters also demanded more political freedom and even asked for direct popular election of the nation's leaders. Clearly this kind of free speech and the Communist system could not exist side by side. As in the Hundred Flowers Campaign of 1956, the Democracy Wall posters were curbed. Many of the activists were arrested and some were jailed.

Today the leaders of China are faced with two main concerns. They must decide what direction China is going to take in the future, and they must also keep a watchful eye on China's borders.

The most sensitive border area, of course, is that with the Soviet Union. Ever since the quarrel between the Chinese and the Soviets in 1960, relations have remained strained and there have been several clashes along the 4000-mile boundary that separates the two nations. At times the Chinese have felt that the threat of a Soviet attack was very close.

Another troublesome spot for China is the offshore island of Taiwan to which the Nationalists fled in 1949. Taiwan is tiny compared with mainland China. It has only 18 million inhabitants versus one billion. Yet the Nationalist leaders of Taiwan—which calls itself the Republic of China—believe that they are the rightful government-in-exile of the giant

People's Republic of China. Taiwan's longtime president, Chiang Kaishek, died in 1975. But his policies were carried on by his son, President Chiang Chingkuo.

The People's Republic does not, of course, agree with the views of the Nationalists on Taiwan. In fact, it counts Taiwan as one of its 22 provinces and claims territorial rights to the island. At times, it has softened its approach and even made friendly offers of reunification. But the chances of finding a means of settling the differences between China and Taiwan seem distant.

In recent times, Taiwan has also been the cause of uneasy relations between China and its newfound friend, the United States. The main reason has been United States' arms sales to Taiwan. Taiwan claims it needs these weapons to defend itself against an attack from the People's Republic.

Also, the United States is a very friendly trading partner of Taiwan. It carries on about twice as much trade with the Taiwanese as it does with the People's Republic of China.

The Chinese leadership, however, hopes it can remain free of any problems abroad so it can pay full attention to matters inside the country. One of the questions for the immediate future seems to be whether China can modernize and still remain a classless society in keeping with Mao's revolutionary ideals.

The answer would seem to be no. In fact, the class system that Mao tried to wipe out is returning. Tens of thousands of educated young Chinese are now going abroad to study. Upon returning to China, these scientists, technical specialists, and intellectuals are becoming a privileged class that will bring about the changes necessary for modernization. Their life-styles are certain to be very different from that of the rice growers and pig breeders of the farming communes.

Another concern of China's leadership is how the less

In spite of recent tensions between China and the United States, Chinese of all ages are seen greeting Americans warmly.

privileged classes will react to these changes. China has too many people and too little to offer them. It has millions of young people who are denied opportunities for advanced schooling and better jobs. Will they become discontented and disloyal? What about the sharp contrast between city and country life? As China modernizes, the cities are sure to further outstrip the countryside as centers of progress. In an attempt to restore a classless society, is it possible that these dissatisfied elements within China might start another Cultural Revolution?

Lastly and most importantly, what about the demands for freedom of political expression like those that appeared briefly on Democracy Wall? Can China find a way within the Communist system to allow its people to express their disagreements with government policy?

Even the most experienced "China watchers" cannot say what the future will bring. As in the past, there will probably be many swings of the pendulum and many changes in direction.

Only one thing is certain. The people of China are amazing in their ability to endure and to adapt. Mao said: "Let the past serve the present." There is no doubt that the Chinese people will find new ways to make the past serve the present— and to invent the future.

Important Dates for China

1700 B.C.	about this time China forms its first dynasty, the Shang
221–207 B.C.	the Qin Dynasty unites the warring states into an empire and builds the Great Wall
206 B.C.–A.D. 221	the Han Dynasty expands the empire under the Confucian system
618–906	under the Tang Dynasty the empire enters its golden age
960–1279	under the Song Dynasty the golden age continues; foot-binding is widely practiced
1279–1368	the Yuan Dynasty of the Mongols is in power; Marco Polo visits China during the reign of the Mongol emperor Kublai Khan
1368–1644	under the Ming Dynasty the Han Chinese are restored to power; during the 1500's Europeans set up trading posts in China and Father Mateo Ricci arrives
1644	the Qing Dynasty of the Manchus comes to power; the pigtail is introduced

120

1781   the British begin selling opium to the Chinese

1839–1842   the First Opium War; Great Britain wins and gets Hong Kong and five new trading ports in China

1844   the United States forces China to sign an unequal treaty and gets special trading privileges

1850   the Taiping Rebellion begins in south China

1856–1860   the Arrow War, or Second Opium War, takes place; the old Summer Palace is looted and burned by British and French troops

1864   the Taiping Heavenly Kingdom is toppled by foreign troops

1893   Mao Zedong is born

1894–1895   the Chino–Japanese War takes place; Japan gets the island of Taiwan and takes control of Korea

1900   the Boxer Rebellion is put down by foreign powers

1908   the Dowager Empress Ci Xi, the last powerful monarch of the Qing Dynasty, dies

1911   October 10, the Nationalist Revolution puts an end to the Qing Dynasty and the Chinese empire

1912   the Republic of China is established with Dr. Sun Yatsen as president

1914–1918   World War I is fought; Germany's territory in China is transferred to Japan

1919   the May Fourth Movement; Nationalists demonstrate against foreign imperialism

1921   July 1, the Chinese Communist Party is formed in Shanghai

1925   Sun Yatsen dies and Chiang Kaishek becomes president of the Republic of China

1927   Chiang Kaishek attacks Communists and drives them into hiding

1931   Japan takes Manchuria from China

1934–1935   the Long March; Mao's forces escape Chiang's blockade and trek north to Yanan

1939–1945   World War II is fought; Japan occupies eastern China and Chiang moves his capital to the interior

1945–1949   civil war takes place between Mao's Communist and Chiang's Kuomintang armies

1949   October 1, the People's Republic of China is established following Chiang Kaishek's flight to the island of Taiwan

1956   the Hundred Flowers Campaign—the people are invited to speak out

1957   the Anti-Rightist Campaign; many who criticized the Communist system are jailed

1958–1960   the Great Leap Forward; agriculture and industry are stepped up for self-sufficiency

1960   the Soviet Union withdraws aid from China following quarrels about Communist policy

1964   Chairman Mao's *Little Red Book,* a collection of his quotations, is published

1966–1969   the Cultural Revolution; the Red Guards persecute "class enemies" in an effort to recapture the spirit of Yanan

1969   Premier Zhou Enlai begins to guide the country toward moderation, but the Gang of Four, led by Mao's wife, continues many of the policies of the Cultural Revolution

1971   China becomes a member of the United Nations after Taiwan loses its seat; the United States Ping-Pong team visits China on first goodwill mission

1972   President Richard M. Nixon of the United States visits China and establishes friendly relations between the two nations

1975   Chiang Kaishek dies on Taiwan; his son Chiang Chingkuo succeeds him as its president

1976   January 8, Zhou Enlai dies; September 9, Mao Zedong dies; Hua Guofeng replaces Mao as Chairman of the Communist Party and the Gang of Four is stripped of its power

1977   Vice-Premier Deng Xiaoping emerges as China's most important political figure and promises the Four Modernizations

1978   wall posters discussing government policy are permitted; China opens itself to international trade and tourism on a major scale

1979   Deng visits the United States; political opinions on wall posters are curbed for having been too outspoken

1981   Hu Yaobang replaces Hua Guofeng as
       Chairman of the Chinese Communist Party

1982   trade relations continue between China and
       the United States, but China is disturbed by
       United States' arms sales to Taiwan; Zhao
       Ziyang, from Deng's home province,
       becomes Prime Minister, or Premier, of
       China; the post of Chairman is abolished
       and Hu Yaobang receives title of General
       Secretary of the Chinese Communist Party

Bibliography

Coye, Molly Joel, and Livingston, Jon, eds. *China, Yesterday and Today.* Rev. ed. New York: Bantam, 1979.

Fraser, John. *The Chinese: Portrait of a People.* New York: Summit Books, Simon and Schuster, 1980.

Galbraith, John. *A Passage to China.* Boston: Houghton Mifflin, 1973.

Galston, Arthur W., with Savage, Jean S. *Daily Life in People's China.* New York: Crowell, 1973.

Lo, Ruth Earnshaw, and Kinderman, Katherine S. *In the Eye of the Typhoon.* New York: Harcourt Brace Jovanovich, 1980.

Loescher, Gil, with Loescher, Ann Dull. *China: Pushing Toward the Year 2000.* New York: Harcourt Brace Jovanovich, 1981.

MacDonald, Malcolm. *Inside China.* Boston: Little, Brown and Co., 1980.

Morath, Inge, and Miller, Arthur. *Chinese Encounters.* New York: Farrar, Straus and Giroux, 1979.

Rius (del Rio, Eduardo). *Mao for Beginners.* New York: Pantheon Books, 1980.

Salisbury, Charlotte. *China Diary: After Mao.* New York: Walker and Co., 1979.

Salisbury, Harrison E. *To Peking—And Beyond: A Report on the New Asia.* New York: Quadrangle, 1973.

SCHELL, ORVILLE. *In the People's Republic.* New York: Random House, 1977.

———. *"Watch Out for the Foreign Guests!": China Encounters the West.* New York: Pantheon Books, 1980.

SIDEL, RUTH. *Families of Fengsheng: Urban Life in China.* Baltimore: Penguin Books, 1974.

TERRILL, ROSS. *Flowers on an Iron Tree.* Boston: Little, Brown and Co., 1975.

———. *The Future of China After Mao.* New York: Delacorte Press, 1978.

WATSON, ANDREW. *Living in China.* Totowa, N.J.: Rowman and Littlefield, 1975.

Index

ABOUT THE AUTHOR

Lila Perl was born and educated in New York City, and she holds a B.A. degree from Brooklyn College. In addition, she has taken graduate work at Teachers College, Columbia University, and at the School of Education, New York University. She is the author of a number of books for adults and for children, both fiction and nonfiction. Several of them concern life in other lands. In preparation for writing them, Miss Perl travels extensively in the country, doing firsthand research and taking many photographs. Her husband, Charles Yerkow, is also a writer, and they live in Beechhurst, New York.